High Stakes
Performance
Assessment

High Stakes Performance Assessment

Perspectives on Kentucky's Educational Reform

Editor
Thomas R. Guskey

CORWIN PRESS, INC.
A Sage Publications Company
Thousand Oaks, California

For information address:

Corwin Press, Inc.
A Sage Publications Company
2455 Teller Road
Thousand Oaks, California 91320

SAGE Publications Ltd.
6 Bonhill Street
London EC2A 4PU
United Kingdom

SAGE Publications India Pvt. Ltd.
M-32 Market
Greater Kailash I
New Delhi 110 048 India

Printed in the United States of America

Library of Congress Cataloging-in-Publication Data

High stakes performance assessment : perspectives on Kentucky's
     educational reform / Thomas R. Guskey, editor.
          p. cm.
     Includes bibliographical references and index.
     ISBN 0–8039–6168–5 (alk. paper) — ISBN 0–8039–6169–3
(pbk. : alk. paper)
     1. Education—Kentucky—Evaluation. 2. Educational Improvement
Act Assessment Program (Ky.) 3. Educational change—Kentucky.
I. Guskey, Thomas R.
LA292.H54   1994
379.1'54—dc20   94–94

94 95 96 97 98 10 9 8 7 6 5 4 3 2 1

Corwin Press Production Editor: Marie Louise Penchoen

Contents

About the Authors

Thomas R. Guskey is professor of Educational Policy Studies and Evaluation at the University of Kentucky. He received his Ph.D. in Measurement, Evaluation, and Statistical Analysis (MESA) from the University of Chicago and has served as a classroom teacher, as a school administrator in the Chicago public schools, and was the first research director of the Center for the Improvement of Teaching and Learning, a national research center located in Chicago. He is the author of over 100 articles and several major books, including *Implementing Mastery Learning* (Wadsworth, 1985) and *Improving Student Learning in College Classrooms* (Charles C Thomas, 1988).

Edward H. Haertel earned his Ph.D. at the University of Chicago in the program on Measurement, Evaluation, and Statistical Analysis (MESA). He is presently professor of Education at Stanford University, where his research and teaching focus on theory, practice, and policy in educational testing and assessment. He is currently investigating the application of new kinds of statistical models to the design and scoring of student performance assessments.

Edward Kifer is professor of Educational Policy Studies and Evaluation at the University of Kentucky. He received his Ph.D. from the University of Chicago, specializing in Measurement, Evaluation, and Statistical Analysis (MESA). He was a Spencer Foundation Fellow at the University of Stockholm where he worked with the International Association for the Evaluation of

Educational Achievement (IEA). He has published numerous articles related to international educational achievement with the most recent being those dealing with IEA's Second Study of Mathematics.

Ben R. Oldham was recently appointed dean of Graduate Education of Georgetown College, Georgetown, Kentucky. Previously, he served as director of Research and Assessment for Fayette County Public Schoools, a school district serving over 30,000 students in Lexington, Kentucky. He received his Ph.D. from the University of Kentucky and has been a high school guidance counselor and physics teacher.

C. Scott Trimble is director of Assessment Implementation in the Office of Curriculum, Assessment, and Accountability of the Kentucky Department of Education. A graduate of Michigan State University, he has worked in the areas of research and student assessment with the Kentucky Department of Education since 1973. His current research interests deal with the impact of assessment policies and the relationship between assessment programs and classroom practice.

Karen Schuster Webb is director of Language Education Programs at the University of Kentucky. A linguist whose research and publications focus on language schemata and pedagogy, as well as multicultural education, she is coauthor of *Speaking and Writing: A Communications Guide for the Professional* (Ginn Press, 1991). She earned her Ph.D. from Indiana University.

Peter Winograd is professor and chair of the Department of Curriculum and Instruction at the University of Kentucky. He received his Ph.D. from the University of Illinois. His research focuses on performance assessment in the areas of reading and writing, helping children become strategic readers, and the cognitive and motivational factors involved in the reading difficulties of children at risk.

Introduction

THOMAS R. GUSKEY

In what has now become an historic decision, the Kentucky Supreme Court ruled in June 1989 that the public school system in the Commonwealth was "unconstitutional." Based on evidence presented in *Rose v. the Council for Better Education, Inc.* (1989), the court concluded that each and every child in the Commonwealth was *not* being provided with an equal opportunity to have an adequate education. The responsibility for providing a system of common schools, according to the court, rested solely with the General Assembly. Therefore, the court ordered the General Assembly to establish a more equitable system and to "monitor it on a continuing basis so that it will always be maintained in a constitutional manner" (*Rose v. the Council for Better Education, Inc.*, 1989).

In response to the court's order, the legislative and executive branches of the state government jointly formed a Task Force on Education Reform, which worked to provide recommendations to the General Assembly. Those recommendations formed the basis of the Kentucky Education Reform Act of 1990.

The Kentucky Education Reform Act, or KERA, represents one of the most comprehensive pieces of educational reform legislation ever enacted in the United States. It addresses nearly every aspect of public education in the Commonwealth, including administration, governance and finance, school organization, accountability, professional development, curriculum, and assessment.

One of the most significant components of KERA is the student assessment program, called the Kentucky Instructional Results Information System (KIRIS). This program is a "high-stakes" assessment program, in that KERA specifies that (a) the results from the assessments will be used to grant rewards to schools that show significant improvement and (b) sanctions will be levied against those that fail to show progress. The high-stakes nature of the assessment program clearly makes KERA an *assessment-driven reform*.

KIRIS is designed to provide evidence on the attainment of six broad learning goals set forth in the reform act. These goals state that students should be able to

1. Use basic communication and math skills for purposes and situations they encounter in life;
2. Apply core concepts and principles from mathematics, the sciences, arts and humanities, social studies, practical-living studies, and vocational studies to purposes and situations they encounter in life;
3. Become self-sufficient individuals;
4. Become responsible members of a family, a work group, or a community;
5. Think and solve problems across the variety of situations they encounter in life; and
6. Connect and integrate the knowledge they have gained in school into their own lives.

Seventy-five learner outcomes, which are currently labeled "learner standards," are specified within these broad learning goals and offer the basis for developing meaningful measures of their attainment.

To assess these broad goals and learner outcomes, a multifaceted, three-phase assessment program was designed. The three phases include the following:

1. Evaluations of portfolios of students' work in the areas of writing and mathematics;

2. Students' performance on a series of "performance events" in the areas of mathematics, science, social studies, arts and humanities, and vocational education or practical living; and

3. Students' scores on "transitional tests," which include both multiple-choice and open-ended items similar to those included in tests used in the National Assessment of Educational Progress. The transitional tests cover the areas of reading, writing, mathematics, science, social studies, arts and humanities, vocational education, or practical living.

Four performance levels are specified in the assessment program: *Novice, Apprentice, Proficient,* and *Distinguished.* KERA specifies that initial administrations of the various phases of the assessment program are to be used to establish baseline data for each school within the Commonwealth. Subsequent administrations are used to document progress, grant awards, and levy sanctions, if necessary.

KERA, and particularly KIRIS, have attracted the attention of many educators and policy makers for two important reasons. One is that, although KERA is not the first reform effort to include a comprehensive assessment system, it is the first one to be driven by assessments that are primarily *performance-based.* The hope of those who developed KERA was that an authentic, performance-based assessment system would compel educators at all levels in the Commonwealth to focus instructional activities on the kinds of higher level skills that will be essential for success in the 21st century. The other reason KERA has attracted so much attention is that it is the first statewide reform effort to make performance-based assessments "high stakes." That is, schools that show significant improvements in KIRIS results will receive financial rewards, whereas those that fail to improve or decline will be subject to severe sanctions. Although concern regarding the most severe sanctions has led to a delay in their imposition, they remain an important part of the law.

The chapters presented in this volume describe a variety of perspectives on KIRIS and its use in an assessment-driven reform effort. From these varied perspectives the rationale for the program is outlined, various facets of the program are examined, and reactions to the program stemming from implementation efforts are described. The individuals presenting these perspectives and interpretations view the program from different levels of education, both within and outside the Commonwealth.

We begin with Edward Kifer, who describes in *Chapter 1* the diverse facets of KIRIS and the rationale behind the development of each. The procedures used in determining the accountability and continuous assessment strands of the program are outlined, along with the process for determining rewards and sanctions. Professor Kifer is intimately familiar with KIRIS, for he was one of five "experts on assessment" selected by the Commonwealth to develop the specifications in the request for proposal that led to the final assessment program contract.

In *Chapter 2*, Peter Winograd and Karen Schuster Webb direct our attention to the impact of high-stakes performance assessments on the ways in which teachers formally and informally assess student learning during day-to-day instruction. They describe the challenges that face classroom teachers as they attempt to develop and to implement instructionally embedded assessments that make up one of the continuous assessment strands of KIRIS. In addition, the sometimes liberating and constricting consequences of KIRIS on instruction are also examined. As leading members of the Department of Curriculum and Instruction at the University of Kentucky, Professors Winograd and Webb know well the impact of KIRIS on classroom teachers and students.

In *Chapter 3*, we turn our focus to the subject of accountability within KIRIS. C. Scott Trimble, director of the Accountability Division in the Office of Assessment and Accountability for the Kentucky Department of Education, describes the many complex issues that are involved in the development of school accountability indexes. The procedures used in KIRIS to set both an accountability baseline and future performance goals for every school in the Commonwealth are outlined. Also discussed are the guidelines that are used to determine the granting of rewards for superior performance and the levying of sanctions for lack of significant progress.

A view of KIRIS from the perspective of a local school district is presented in *Chapter 4*. Ben R. Oldham, former director of Testing and Evaluation for Fayette County Public Schools, one of the largest school districts in the Commonwealth, describes the local impact of the move from traditional norm-referenced tests to mandated, high-stakes performance-based assessments. Included is a discussion of public relations campaigns, professional development efforts, and implications for classroom practice.

Finally, in *Chapter 5*, Edward H. Haertel presents an overview of the many facets of KIRIS and discusses the broader implications of the program for both researchers and practitioners. He not only offers several keen insights to potentially troublesome aspects of the program but also suggests how these might be resolved. Professor Haertel has been a close observer of the program since its inception and also serves on the Technical Advisory Committee for Advanced Systems in Measurement and Evaluation, Inc., the contractual developer for KIRIS.

Our intention in this book is not only to clarify the various dimensions of one of the nation's most ambitious statewide student assessment programs but also to provide a variety of diverse views of that program and its impact on educational practice. Above all, we hope it illustrates the tremendous complexity of the issues involved when performance-based assessments are employed in a high-stakes context and the implications of such assessments for educators at different levels.

It should be noted that as implementation proceeds, various aspects of the program are continually revised. As a result, current practice may differ somewhat from what the authors have described. Furthermore, in many cases the answers to questions raised by the authors remain unanswered. Nevertheless, we hope that our efforts to lay bare those questions will be helpful to all those who are currently struggling to find better and more meaningful ways to assess student learning for the purpose of improving the teaching and learning process.

Reference

Rose v. Council for Better Education, Inc., KY 88-SC-804-TG, (Sept 28, 1989).

ONE

Development of the Kentucky Instructional Results Information System (KIRIS)

EDWARD KIFER

The Legislation

As was discussed in the Introduction, the Kentucky Education Reform Act (KERA) was passed by the General Assembly in 1990 in response to a legal opinion that declared Kentucky's system of public education to be unconstitutional. A major component of the reform act, House Bill 940, Section I, contains specifications for statewide assessments of student performance relative to defined learner outcomes. In addition, this bill contains other mandates regarding the performance assessments. For example, there are goal statements, specifications of general outcomes, and mandates for continuous assessment. Performance assessments play a central role in KERA. They are the operational measures of goals defined by the Council on School Performance Standards that reflect the learning outcomes required of all Kentucky students.

Performance demonstrations of these outcomes are to be the most heavily weighted component of a statewide, school-level, accountability system. They also are to be powerful enough to change instructional patterns. That is, the mandated continuous assessment program was to be designed so that instruction and assessment become "seamless."

Procedures for Implementing Performance Assessments

Several portions of House Bill 940 pertain to developing and implementing the statewide performance assessment system. The Council on School Performance Standards framed six broad learning goals for Kentucky education. By means of a series of committees, expected, measurable learner outcomes were to be defined, based on these goals. The State Board for Elementary and Secondary Education was then to disseminate to local districts and schools a model curriculum framework tied directly to the broad goals, the learner outcomes, and the assessment strategies. The board was also responsible for creating and implementing the assessment system. The full assessment system, containing an interim testing program, a continuous assessment program, and a program of school accountability was to be in place no later than the 1995/1996 school year.

The interim testing program was to begin in the spring of 1992. This program was to address the areas of reading, mathematics, writing, science, and social science for students in Grades 4, 8, and 12. It was to be designed to provide national comparisons as well as accountability information. According to the law, this testing program was to be similar to the National Assessment of Educational Progress. It was to be administered to a sample of students representative of each school in the Commonwealth. As will be discussed later, these interim tests also contained a variety of measures, including transitional items and tasks, performance events, and portfolio tasks. Performance on these cognitive measures then would be used, along with other factors, to establish a performance baseline for each school in the Commonwealth to be used for accountability purposes.

Designing the Statewide Assessment

The State Board for Elementary and Secondary Education hired five national consultants, known for their expertise in assessment of student learning, to design the assessment system.

The consultants included Pat Forgione of the State Department of Education in Connecticut, Edward Kifer of the University of Kentucky, Jason Millman from Cornell University, Doris Redfield of the University of California at Los Angeles (UCLA) Center for the Study of Evaluation, and Grant Wiggins of CLASS (Center on Learning, Assessment, and School Structure, a nonprofit education organization in Geneseo, New York). The first task of this group was to prepare a request for proposal that could be responded to by potential contractors.

The Request for Proposal and the Contractor

The request for proposal (RFP) contained the design of the assessment program as envisioned by five consultants. The first five figures in this chapter come directly from that RFP. Six potential contractors responded to the RFP. Based on an extensive review of the contractors' proposals, the consultants recommended to the State Board for Elementary and Secondary Education that Advanced Systems, Inc. be awarded the contract, and the board agreed.

The Assessment Design

Figure 1.1 captures the assessment scheme envisioned by the consultants. As shown in the figure, the assessment program is embedded in the Commonwealth's six broad learning goals as defined in the law and made operational by the Council on School Performance Standards. The program contains two major strands: the accountability assessment and the continuous assessment.

Accountability Strand

According to the law, each school in the Commonwealth must participate in the accountability strand. There are three components in this assessment strand: (a) performance measurements,

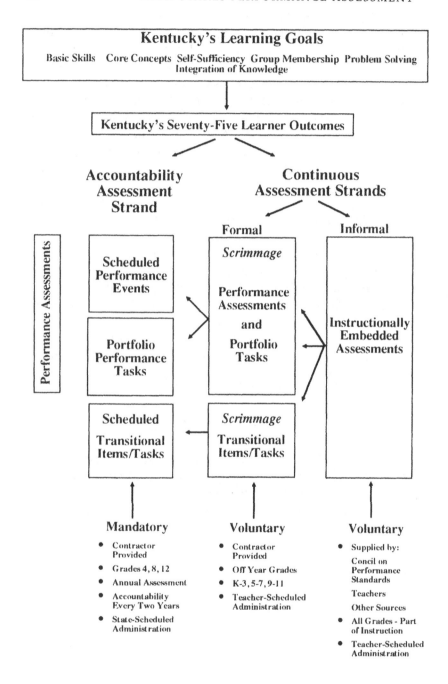

Figure 1.1. Accountability and Continuous Assessment Strands

(b) portfolio tasks, and (c) transitional items and tasks. Although assessment in this strand is conducted annually, the accountability decision is made every 2 years.

Continuous Assessment Strand

The continuous assessment strand has two components, both of which are voluntary. The formal component is designed to give students in grades other than Grades 4, 8, and 12 an opportunity to practice the types of activities required in the accountability strand. Advanced Systems, Inc. is required to provide those practice materials and activities to schools that wish to purchase them. The second component of continuous assessment is related to day-by-day activities within classrooms. Here, the kinds of products, performances, and activities that are part of a school's instructional program are meant to be indistinguishable from the formal assessment activities conducted annually in the accountability assessments. Students and teachers at all grade levels should be working together on things quite similar to what will be required in the assessment program. It was envisioned that teachers would be given exemplary materials from the Council on School Performance Standards and use what is already being done to make instruction and assessment appear to be inextricably intertwined.

The School as the Unit for Improvement

Although the reform act states the strong expectation that each child can learn and learn at a high level, schools, not individuals, are the units that are expected to improve. Also according to the law, that improvement must be demonstrated every 2 years. Improvement is expected in not only cognitive areas measured by the performance assessments and more traditional tests but also in areas such as attendance, dropout rates, transitions from school, and expectations for achievement. School improvement is defined in the law as the change in the percentage of successful students over time. As indicated below, it is a composite of outcomes that are weighted to get this percentage of successful students.

School Accountability

During the spring of 1992, schools throughout the Commonwealth were measured through a variety of means in order to establish a baseline from which to judge improvement. Two years later they will be held accountable for an increase in the percentage of successful students. Schools can be rewarded or sanctioned on the basis of their performance during the 2-year period. Students in Grades 4, 8, or 12 are used for purposes of accountability. The continuous assessment part of the legislation, however, is applicable to every grade level.

Figure 1.2 depicts the accountability system. The contractor, Advanced Systems, Inc., was required to develop a formula that weights the six learning goals to arrive at a composite percentage of successful students in a school. That composite was, by law, to give more weight to the cognitive goal than to any of the other five goals. The estimated percentage of successful students in a school in the spring of 1992 is the Time 1 baseline for a school. Each school is then expected to improve given its initial status; that is, from its Time 1 baseline.

The contractor was also to calculate a threshold value for each school that represents its target for improvement during the 2-year accountability cycle. The threshold was to be defined so that it was fair to each school, regardless of its initial status. In other words, a school with a high proportion of successful students would not be expected to improve as much as one with a lower percentage of successful students.

In 1994, at the end of the 2-year cycle, an accountability decision is to be made and a new threshold, based on a new percentage of successful students, will be estimated for each school. Schools that exceed their threshold or target values by 1% or more are eligible for financial rewards. Schools that have a percentage of successful students at or below their baseline are to be sanctioned. A decrease in the percentage of successful students of up to 5% places the school in a category where improvement is needed. Those schools must develop a school improvement plan, are eligible to receive additional funding, and are assisted by a group of distinguished educators. A decrease of more than 5%

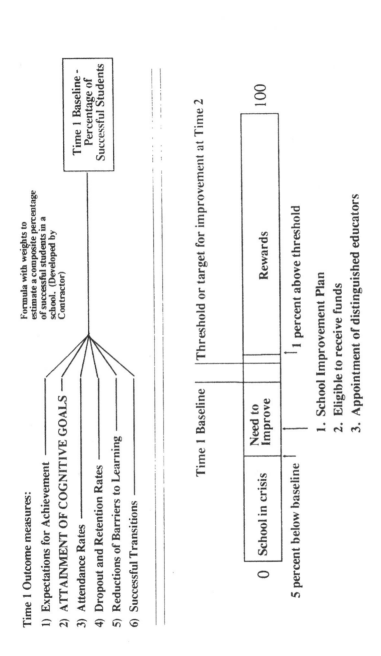

Time 1 Outcome measures:

1) Expectations for Achievement
2) ATTAINMENT OF COGNITIVE GOALS
3) Attendance Rates
4) Dropout and Retention Rates
5) Reductions of Barriers to Learning
6) Successful Transitions

Formula with weights to estimate a composite percentage of successful students in a school. (Developed by Contractor)

Time 1 Baseline - Percentage of Successful Students

Threshold or target for improvement at Time 2

100

Rewards

1 percent above threshold

1. School Improvement Plan
2. Eligible to receive funds
3. Appointment of distinguished educators

Time 1 Baseline

Need to Improve

0   School in crisis

5 percent below baseline

Figure 1.2. Determining Rewards and Sanctions

places a school in a crisis category. Sanctions for a school *in crisis* include placing the State Department of Education in control of the school.

It should be noted that there is ambiguity in the law with regard to these levels. As stated above, the law indicates there is no penalty for a school that exceeds its baseline but does not reach its threshold. Advanced Systems, Inc. has in its work, however, defined that area as one where sanctions occur.

Broadening the Assessment Over Time

Both prudence and the law suggest that a system so complex as this must be implemented in stages. Because, again by law, the full assessment system must be in place by 1996, the RFP suggests three ways in which the assessment could expand over time.

The first is in terms of the components of the accountability strand. Figure 1.3 shows one way in which that expansion could occur. The length of the bars depict the size of the assessment increasing over time. Consistent with the legislation, more performance events and portfolio tasks are included in the assessments in each subsequent year. Also, the proportion of those types of activities increases each year. Advanced Systems, Inc. can choose, of course, to alter the proportions.

Figure 1.4 shows another kind of expansion over time. The interim testing represents a small part of what the accountability strand is in 1996. Again, consistent with the law, the interim testing is part of the Time 1 baseline. There is an increasing emphasis on performance assessment, and the baseline, or that for which schools are held accountable, expands dramatically from 1992 to 1996.

Figure 1.5 represents yet another kind of expansion of the assessment system. In 1992, there are limited assessments based on five content areas and three goal areas. By 1996, each of the relevant content areas and each of the goals are a part of the assessment system.

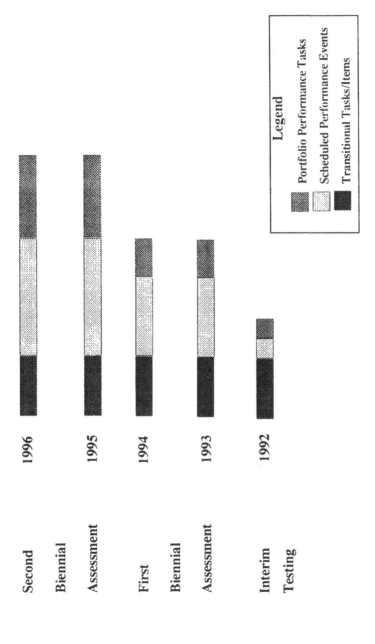

Figure 1.3. Relative Emphasis of Task Types Over Time

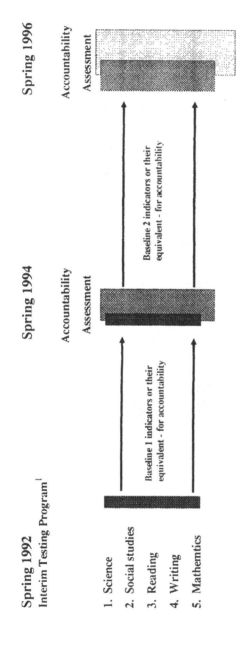

Spring 1992
Interim Testing Program[1]

1. Science
2. Social studies
3. Reading
4. Writing
5. Mathemtics

Baseline 1 indicators or their
equivalent - for accountability

Spring 1994

Accountability

Assessment

Baseline 2 indicators or their
equivalent - for accountability

Spring 1996

Accountability

Assessment

[1]**Notes - Interim Testing**

A. An interim testing program must include each of the above five areas.

B. A variety of measurement procedures may be used at this time. Performance assessments are to be
included with emphasis increasing across time.

C. Accountability is measured, in part, by the change in performance on the cognitive indicators
connected by the arrows.

D. The baseline is expected to get wider over time -- i.e., include more cognitive areas.

E. A continuous assessment component is on-going but not shown.

Figure 1.4. The Interim Testing Program, Expanding Baselines and Accountability

Years	1992	1993 1994	1995 1996
Goals	Limited Assessments	Wider Assessments	Extensive Assessments
b1-Basic Skills	Writing	Writing	Writing
		Reading	Reading
	Reading	Mathematics	Mathematics
		Social Science	Social Science
	Mathematics	Science	Science
h2-Core Concepts	Social Science		
		Arts/Humanities	Arts/Humanities
		Practical Living	Practical Living
	Science	Vocational Education	Vocational Education
h5-Problem Solving			
			Selected
			Valued
			Outcomes
h3-Self-Sufficiency			Related
			to:
			Self-Sufficiency
h4-Group Membership			
			Group Membership
h6-Integration			Integration of Knowledge

Figure 1.5. Performance Assessments of Kentucky's Valued Outcomes Increasing Over Time

Concluding Remarks

Kentucky's assessment system is large, complex, and ambitious. It aims to do two, perhaps incompatible, things: first, to provide a statewide, school-level accountability system; and second, to produce dramatic changes in curriculum and instruction in public schools. In terms of the latter, it is based on the premise that exemplary assessment procedures will produce optimal instruction. Teaching to the assessments, it is believed, will not only produce increasingly higher test scores but will also drive desirable instructional practices.

So far, it appears that more emphasis has been placed on the accountability portion of the assessment system than on either of the components of continuous assessment. Because increasingly higher proportions of the assessments will be either performance tasks or portfolios, it is crucial that teachers be trained to conduct these and to use them routinely in their classrooms.

The first segment of the assessment program was conducted in the spring of 1992. As the assessment program progresses through the decade, we will begin to see if a major reform effort, driven in large part by a multidimensional student performance assessment program, can be successful in bringing about the kinds of improvement intended.

TWO

Impact on Curriculum and Instruction Reform

PETER WINOGRAD and KAREN SCHUSTER WEBB

The Kentucky Education Reform Act (KERA) called for profound changes in what and how children are taught; in the support systems available to students, families, teachers, and schools; in how schools are governed; and in how the system of public education is financed. Each of the many different strands of KERA, however, had helping Kentucky students become more prepared for life beyond the walls of the classroom as its ultimate goal.

Six goals were developed as part of the reform that identify what all students should know and be able to do. These goals include the following:

1. Students should be able to use basic communication and math skills for purposes and situations they encounter in life.
2. Students should be able to apply core concepts and principles from mathematics, the sciences, arts and humanities, social studies, practical-living studies, and vocational studies for purposes and situations they encounter in life.
3. Students should become self-sufficient individuals.
4. Students should become responsible members of a family, a work group, or a community.
5. Students should be able to think and solve problems across the variety of situations they encounter in life.

6. Students should be able to connect and integrate the knowledge they have gained in school into their own lives.

From these six broad learning goals were derived 75 learner outcomes that provide a more specific and measurable description of what students should know and be able to do. For example, a learner outcome in reading is, "Students construct meaning from a variety of print materials for a variety of purposes through reading." Similarly, one of the learner outcomes for writing is, "Students communicate ideas and information to a variety of audiences for a variety of purposes in a variety of modes through writing."

The six learning goals and the 75 learner outcomes provide the basis for the changes in curriculum and instruction that are to occur in elementary, middle, and high schools across the Commonwealth as a result of KERA. But how are these changes to be made? And once made, how do we know if they are making a difference in what students know and are able to do? In short, how do we know if the reforms are effective?

The purpose of this chapter is to focus on some of the issues that Kentucky educators face as they attempt to answer these crucial questions. We begin with a brief overview of the assessment program, called the *Kentucky Instructional Results Information System* (KIRIS). Next, we focus on six issues that emerge as educators attempt to reform assessment. Finally, we turn to a case study of how one group of primary teachers successfully addressed these issues as they developed an alternative format for reporting student learning to parents.

KIRIS: An Overview

As KERA was taking shape, the Kentucky Council on School Performance Standards recommended that a major effort be launched to assess student performance beyond what could be measured by paper- and-pencil tests (Council on School Performance Standards, 1989). Specifically, the council recommended the Commonwealth establish a two-pronged assessment initiative.

One part of the initiative would focus on developing a statewide method for ensuring local school accountability for student achievement. The second part would focus on helping local schools enhance their ability to use ongoing student assessment to improve instruction. This distinction between assessment for accountability and assessment for instruction is one of the most important aspects of Kentucky's efforts to reform assessment.

The other chapters in this book describe the development and rationale of KIRIS in detail. For the purposes of this chapter, however, it is important to understand that the assessment system contains three interrelated strands. These are illustrated in chapter 1, Figure 1.1.

The focus of this chapter is on the third strand— those kinds of assessments that are informal and instructionally embedded. In the previous chapter, Kifer referred to these kinds of assessments as the second component of the continuous assessment strand dealing most closely with day-to-day instruction. If these day-to-day kinds of assessments are designed thoughtfully, then assessment and instruction can truly become "seamless."

Instructionally embedded assessments are a subset of what is often referred to in the current literature as "authentic" or "alternative" assessments (e.g., Maeroff, 1991; Wiggins, 1989). They are primarily used for purposes of instruction rather than for accountability and can encompass a wide array of instruments, techniques, and approaches. They include, for example, portfolios, anecdotal records, observational checklists, paper- and-pencil tests, report cards, and rating scales. Assessments such as these can be used throughout the year according to teachers' schedules. In addition, they often are developed by teachers rather than by psychometricians or commercial test publishers.

Assessment for Instruction: Problems Worth Solving

Teachers who struggle to develop instructionally embedded assessments (what we refer to as alternative assessments) face six major problems. If these can be successfully resolved, we are convinced the result will be assessments that enhance students' understanding of themselves and their world, rather than simply measure learning in a narrow sense.

Problem 1: Clarifying the Goals of Assessment

When teachers begin developing alternative assessments, they first must consider what they want to measure. Identifying what is to be measured, however, is no easy task.

One way to conceptualize this problem is to think of a continuum that ranges from goals that are broad and general to goals that are extremely narrow and specific. For example, the learning goal, "Students should be able to use basic communication and math skills for purposes and situations they encounter in life," is a very general goal. Although obviously important, it is too broad to measure in any practical way. The goal, "Students construct meaning from a variety of print materials for a variety of purposes through reading," is less general and would be somewhat easier to measure. The goal, "Students should identify the sound the letter *a* represents in the word *man*," is an example of a very specific goal that is easy to measure but of questionable importance.

Educators often identify broad, meaningful goals as they develop their curriculum but then employ a more traditional form of assessment, typically a standardized achievement test. As a result, the test maker's goals become the de facto goals of instruction. Thus, even though the curriculum identifies the ability to apply communication in real life as the goal, students are evaluated based on their ability to read short paragraphs and to select correct answers to questions stated in a multiple-choice format.

It is very important that the goals identified in the curriculum are the same goals addressed in the assessment. This point is crucial in Kentucky where the stated goals are so different from those typically assessed in standardized instruments.

Problem 2: Clarifying the Audiences to Be Addressed

Assessment can and should serve different purposes (Winograd, Paris, & Bridge, 1991). We find it useful to think about the various purposes of assessment in terms of different audiences. For example, assessment can help

- Students become more self-reflective and in control of their own learning
- Teachers focus their instruction more effectively
- Educators determine which students are eligible for Chapter 1, programs for the gifted, or special education
- Parents understand more about their children's progress as learners
- Administrators understand how groups of students in their schools are progressing as learners
- Legislators and other representatives of the public understand how cohorts of students across the state are progressing as learners

Each of these audiences is important and worthy of the best information available. It is also clear, however, that no single instrument or approach will adequately fulfill the needs of all these audiences.

Problem 3: Selecting and Developing Assessment Techniques and Tasks

If traditional multiple-choice tests are considered inadequate, what techniques and tasks should be used in their place? A growing body of literature exists today on alternative methods of assessments (e.g., Harp, 1991; Johnston, 1992; Kemp, 1989; Tierney, Carter, & Desai, 1991). These methods include portfolios, anecdotal checklists, developmental checklists, rating scales, student-teacher conferences, parent-teacher conferences, narrative report cards, and a variety of performance-based assessments. The key to selecting and developing alternative assessment techniques is to have a clear idea of the goals to be evaluated and the audiences to be addressed.

Suppose, for example, that a teacher decides that developing students' ability to evaluate their own writing is an important

Name _____ Date _____

I just looked in my best pieces folder! I read some stories and looked at my writing since the beginning of school. How have I improved as a writer?

_____

_____

_____

_____

What are some things I can do now that I could not do at the beginning of school?

_____

_____

_____

_____

What am I going to work on?

_____

_____

_____

_____

Figure 2.1. Checklist for Self-Evaluation

instructional goal and that the students themselves are the audience. An appropriate assessment method in this case may be simply a checklist that students can use to reflect on their written work. Two examples are shown in Figures 2.1 and 2.2.

Problem 4: Setting Standards of Student Performance

Whereas gathering information on students' performance through portfolios, observations, conferences, and other forms of alternative assessment may be relatively easy, interpreting this information can be challenging.

In the past, educators relied on constructs such as grade equivalents, age equivalents, percentile scores, or standard scores to measure student growth. The limitations of these traditional constructs,

1. Did I think about my audience?

2. Did I think about my purpose?

3. Will my work make sense to my audience?

4. Did I make my point?

5. Did I include the important details?

6. Are my ideas in a logical order?

7. Do my sentences express complete thoughts?

8. Did I choose good words?

9. Did I check my spelling?

10. Is my punctuation correct?

NAME _____

Figure 2.2. Writer's Self-Evaluation

however, are well-known (e.g., Guskey & Kifer, 1990; Haney & Madaus, 1989; Neill & Medina, 1989; Shepard, 1989). Although their meaning seemed explicit, they were rarely understood correctly by students, their parents, teachers, or administrators.

One way to deal with the issue of standards when using alternative forms of assessment is to develop scoring rubrics with performance levels. Rubrics are specific guidelines that can be used to describe students' work in reading, writing, mathematics, and other content areas. Many of the scoring rubrics used in KIRIS, for example, employ a 4-point scale to rate the quality of students' work. These rubrics contain words and phrases that describe the characteristics of each point on the scale. The scorer then compares the work being evaluated to the descriptions or examples contained in the rubric. Rubrics are particularly useful because they help students, teachers, and parents gain a better understanding of what is expected.

Rubrics also play a crucial role in both the accountability and instructionally embedded strands of KIRIS. For purposes of accountability, student performance is defined in terms of four performance levels:

Novice: The student is beginning to show an understanding of new information or skills.

Apprentice: The student has gained more understanding and can complete some important parts of the task.

Proficient: The student understands the major concepts, can do almost all of the task, and can communicate concepts clearly.

Distinguished: The student has a deep level of understanding of the concept or process and can complete all important parts of the task. The student can communicate well and offer insightful interpretations or extensions (generalizations, applications, and analogies).

Using rubrics and setting standards with performance levels has several advantages over traditional methods such as letter grades, grade equivalents, or percentile scores. First, standards of performance are based on clear and consistent criteria that can be applied across contexts. In contrast, the criteria for getting an "A" may vary from one school to another. Grade equivalents and percentile scores likewise provide little, if any, information about the criteria used for evaluation. Second, scoring rubrics and performance levels emphasize the developmental nature of learning. Describing a student as a "novice," for example, implies that the student has room to grow. In contrast, giving a student an "F" communicates only that the student is a failure.

Problem 5: Establishing Methods of Management

Perhaps the most difficult problem teachers face when they consider alternative forms of assessment is finding ways to manage all the information. Gathering and interpreting this evidence takes time and careful thought. One way to make alternative assessments more manageable is to ensure that they replace traditional assessments rather than simply add to the burden of testing. Unfortunately, at the present time in Kentucky, many teachers find themselves dealing with traditional standardized tests in addition to the new statewide assessments that include portfolios, anecdotal records, conferences, and other forms of instructionally embedded assessments. In a primary classroom, for example, 6-

and 7-year-old children may spend 8 days or more taking the *Comprehensive Test of Basic Skills* and the new state performance assessments.

Another way to make alternative assessments more manageable is to provide teachers with adequate training (e.g., Maeroff, 1991; Winograd & Jones, 1992). If teachers are to use portfolios efficiently, they need to know a great deal about how children learn, effective instructional practices, and the construction, management, and interpretation of portfolios.

Alternative assessments can also be made more manageable by providing teachers with time and support for collaboration with their colleagues. Teachers are generally more successful in using alternative assessments when they have opportunities to plan together for implementation.

Embedding assessment tasks within instructional activities is yet another way to make management easier. The advantage of integrating assessment with instruction is that time is not taken away from teaching. This is a complex issue, and we shall examine it in more detail next.

Problem 6: Integrating Assessment and Instruction

Traditional methods of assessment are often criticized as not being aligned with what is taught during good instruction. To embed assessment within instruction requires a clear understanding of what is involved in good instruction.

The six learning goals identified in KERA provide a basis for how good instruction is defined (e.g., EdNews, 1992). Specifically, good instruction in Kentucky

- Assumes that students are active creators of meaning
- Involves high expectations for all students
- Integrates writing across the curriculum
- Encourages students to become proficient at using reading, writing, mathematics, and other basic skills in all areas of the curriculum
- Is focused on the ability to apply what has been learned to real-life problems

- Encourages student inquiry and exploration
- Involves students in hands-on investigations and interpretative discussions
- Uses a variety of materials, including print, software, and other resources
- Groups students flexibly based on interests, work habits, learning needs, or the nature of the task
- Is focused on concepts, important skills in authentic contexts, processes, and attitudes
- Integrates or correlates content areas when appropriate
- Involves students in collaborative learning

Defining good instruction and putting these precepts into practice is but part of what it takes to integrate instruction and assessment. Teachers also need to identify what products, work samples, artifacts, processes, behaviors, or other kinds of evidence should be gathered during instruction for the purposes of assessment. Developmental checklists, rating scales, guidelines for portfolios, and scoring rubrics provide teachers with guidance about the kinds of evidence worth gathering during instruction.

Another step in the process of integrating instruction and assessment is interpretation of the evidence and its use to enrich the next set of lessons. In short, embedding assessment in instruction means that the assessment provides evidence to guide further learning. This concept is not new, of course, but it remains challenging, especially as educators move beyond teaching and testing low-level skills to focus on more complex and meaningful student outcomes.

In summary, these six problems—clarifying the goals of assessment, clarifying the audiences to be addressed, selecting and developing the assessment techniques, setting standards of student performance, establishing methods of management, and integrating instruction and assessment—must be addressed as teachers move forward in implementing the continuous assessment strand of KIRIS. Next, we examine how one group of primary teachers handled these problems as they developed new approaches to classroom assessment.

Solving Problems in a Primary Classroom: A Case Study

One of the most sweeping aspects of KERA is the mandate that kindergarten, first, second, and third grades be combined into an ungraded primary program in which children of more than one age are placed into multiage, multiability classrooms. Seven critical attributes of successful ungraded primary programs have been identified by the Kentucky Department of Education (*The Wonder Years*, 1991). These include the following:

Developmentally appropriate practices: This curriculum addresses the physical, social, intellectual, emotional, aesthetic, or artistic needs of young children and permits them to progress through an integrated curriculum at their own rate.

Multiage and multiability classrooms: These are classrooms where flexible grouping and regrouping of children of different ages, sex, and abilities takes place. In addition, children may be assigned to the same teacher(s) for more than 1 year.

Continuous progress: Students will progress through the primary program at their own rate without comparison to the rates of others or consideration of the number of years in school.

Authentic assessment: This assessment occurs continually in the context of the learning environment and reflects actual learning experiences that can be documented through observation, anecdotal records, journals, logs, work samples, conferences, and other methods.

Qualitative reporting: Children's progress is communicated to families through various home-school methods of communication that focus on the growth and development of the whole child.

Professional teamwork: All professional staff members communicate and plan on a regular basis to meet the needs of groups as well as individual children.

Positive parent involvement: This concerns relationships between school and home, individuals, or groups that enhance communication, promote understanding, and increase opportunities for children to experience success.

These seven critical attributes provide a sense of what is expected from teachers in the primary program. The case study described here focuses on the experiences of four teachers who sought to implement these attributes in one Kentucky elementary school.

The efforts of these teachers began with the development of a report card for the parents of children in the primary program. Prior to transition to the primary program, they used a report card with a traditional format. The use of alternative methods of assessment, however, required a reporting system more congruent with their instruction. Figure 2.3 contains an example of the report card they devised.

In developing this report card, the teachers focused on the needs of *parents* as the audience. They knew that parents need some sense of how their children are progressing on important instructional goals. The teachers also realized that qualitative reporting is a critical attribute of a successful primary program. The blank spaces on the first and second pages of the form allow teachers to write narrative comments about individual children. Some examples of the kinds of comments these teachers wrote about their students include the following:

> I love having reading conferences with Tom. He has really begun to be able to discuss a book. He comprehends the story well. We discussed character feelings in Fuzzy Rabbit. He is excellent at reading silently to answer content questions. His oral reading is very fluent and improved.

> Jenny says she likes looking at books and reading, but she doesn't like to read at home. She would be helped a great deal if she would just read 10 minutes a night (read *to* her). Her goal in reading is to "get books she could read."

Qualitative reporting calls for extensive home-school communication. This type of communication must flow between the teacher and the family, not just from the teacher to the family. The opportunity for parent responses provides teachers with important insights about students and their families. Thus these teachers included a space on the report card for parents to write a home goal for their child. The following are examples from different parents:

> My goals for L is to have more individual time with her, to have her read to me more, and to let her help me cook more (she likes that). She and I made banana bread a few weeks ago. She helped me follow the recipe, get ingredients prepared, and clean up. We had a good time.

> I don't know what's happening, but A's not wanting to go to school now, he says he is bored. He has been complaining for about the last two weeks. I told him to talk to you but, of course, he won't. I don't know what to do.

> I let B know that I am very proud of him. He has done very good. My home goal is to help B with his behavior and working with others. Thank you.

The teachers spent a great deal of time considering the goals they wanted to include on their report card. Their final choices focused on two levels of the continuum from broad goals down to specific skills. They first identified four broad areas of language and literacy, math, listening and speaking, and personal and social growth. These are key areas in a developmentally appropriate curriculum. Then, within each of the four areas, they identified specific instructional goals that were both meaningful and measurable.

Many of the specific goals they chose reveal an insightful approach to solving the problems of selecting assessment tasks and integrating instruction with assessment. For example, the goal "During Super Silent Reading the student involves self intensely with print" is an important goal that is directly tied to a key instructional activity in teaching reading in a whole language classroom. Integrating assessment with instructional activities enables the teachers to observe students and gather crucial information for evaluation at the same time they are engaged in meaningful instruction.

Saffell Street School
Primary Progress Report

Student _____   Teacher _____

LANGUAGE AND LITERACY

DISPLAYS INTEREST IN PRINT
_____ shares books with others
_____ chooses to spend time with books
_____ asks to be read to
_____ listens attentively to books in a group
_____ contributes to group discussion
_____ checks out books frequently

DURING SUPER SILENT READING

Involves self intensely with print	Maintains interest in print with additional support	Has difficulty being involved with print

DURING GROUP READING

Totally involved with reading experiences	Willing to participate with additional support	Unable to stay involved with group activity

DURING READING DISCUSSIONS

Carries on a meaningful conversation about reading	Willing to answer questions about reading material with guidance	Unable to express thoughts or feelings about reading material

DISPLAYS INTEREST IN WRITING
_____ chooses to write or draw
_____ wants more writing time
_____ wants to share their writing
_____ shows interest in others' writing
_____ uses available print

DURING WRITING WORKSHOP

Shows independence using the writing process	Shows some independence, needing individual guidance to progress	Needs individual guidance to participate

STORY DEVELOPMENT

Develops and organizes ideas with a purpose	Expresses logical and sequential thoughts and ideas; needs to develop a clearer purpose	Expresses ideas; may or may not be logically connected

KNOWLEDGE OF MECHANICS

Able to use punctuation, capitals, grammar and complete sentences	Shows some use of punctuation, capitals, grammar and complete sentences, but not consistently	Needs awareness of punctuation, capitals, grammar and complete sentences

READING STRATEGIES (e.g. picture clues, context, background knowledge, prediction, phonics)

Uses a variety of reading strategies	Beginning to use one or more reading strategies	Unaware of reading strategies

STEPS IN READING
_____ listening to stories, unaware of print and its function
_____ picture reading, describing pictures
_____ pretends reading, turning pages, tracking print, rehearsing silently
_____ memory reading
_____ recognizes some words but not all
_____ recognizes patterns in reading
_____ reading with understanding, summarizes

Figure 2.3. Saffell Street School Primary Progress Report

Student _____   Date _____

MATH

PROBLEM SOLVING

Able to problem solve independently	Can use problem solving with some guidance	Needs assistance to solve problems

COMMUNICATES MEANING

Using symbols and words to show meaning	Using symbols and/or words, needing assistance to show meaning	Needs assistance to use symbols and/or words to show meaning

NUMBER UNDERSTANDING

Demonstrates and extends under-standing about number meaning	Demonstrates understanding about number meaning	Beginning to show an awareness of number meaning

LISTENING AND SPEAKING

FOLLOWS DIRECTIONS

Almost always follows directions independently	Working to develop better listening skills to follow through with directions	Needs constant assistance in following directions

COMMUNICATES IDEAS VERBALLY

Willing and able to communicate effectively with others	Willing to express thoughts; working to develop a clearer focus	Needs encourage-ment to express ideas

PERSONAL AND SOCIAL GROWTH

USE OF TIME

Is productive and involved	Sometimes needs encouragement to use time productively	Needs assistance to become involved in productive activities

EFFECTIVE GROUP MEMBER

Works well with others	Needs limited assistance to work with others	Has difficulty working with others

COOPERATES WITH PEERS AND SCHOOL PERSONNEL

Shows respect and gets along well with others	Needs encourage-ment with limited guidance	Needs constant reminding of how to cooperate

Parents! Please write a home goal for your child. It may be something that you will continue to work on during this next reporting period.

Sign and return _____   Date _____

The issue of setting standards for student performance was approached through the use of rubrics, observational checklists, and developmental scales. The rubric for "During Reading Discussion," for example, required the development of a 3-point scale that clearly communicates how students are progressing in this important aspect of schooling.

During Reading Discussion

Independent	Developing	Beginning
Carries on a meaningful conversation about reading material	Willing to answer questions about reading material with guidance	Unable to express thoughts or feelings about reading material

The continuum represented under this goal helps parents understand the developmental behaviors teachers are looking for as students grow. *Beginning* students are unable to clearly express their thoughts about what they have read. *Developing* students can answer questions about what they have read, but teachers still must provide some modeling and support. *Independent* students can discuss what they have read with ease and confidence.

The goal "Displays Interest in Print" contains an example of an observational checklist. Sharing books with others, choosing to spend time with books, asking to be read to, and the other behaviors on this checklist are the kinds of evidence that teachers use to evaluate whether children are developing an interest in reading.

An example of a developmental scale is included under the label *Steps in Reading*. Helping parents understand that children generally move from simply listening to stories to reading on their own with understanding is one way to communicate a student's progress and growth in literacy.

Finally, the Primary Progress Report developed by these teachers is manageable. As they go about their daily instruction, these teachers observe their students, engage in conversations with them, and gather samples of their work. They use the rubrics, the observational checklists, and the developmental scales as a guide both in gathering information and in interpreting students' performance. The information gathered during instruction is also used on the report card to communicate to parents.

Conclusion

Clarifying the goals of assessment, focusing on the needs of a specific audience, developing meaningful assessment tasks and techniques, setting standards for student performance, making the whole process manageable, and integrating assessment with instruction are some of the challenges that face Kentucky educators as they attempt to implement the reforms in assessment mandated by KERA. Fortunately, our experience and evidence indicates that educators throughout the Commonwealth have the vision, the commitment, and the tenacity to meet these challenges in ways that will help all children grow to their fullest potential.

References

Council on School Performance Standards. (1989). *Preparing Kentucky youth for the next century: What students should know and be able to do and how learning should be assessed.* Paducah: Western Kentucky University.

EdNews. (1992). *Teaching, learning, assessment: Transforming the classroom.* Frankfort: Kentucky Department of Education.

Guskey, T. R., & Kifer, E. (1990). Ranking school districts on the basis of statewide test results: It is meaningful or misleading? *Educational Measurement: Issues and Practice, 9*(1), 11-16.

Haney, W., & Madaus, G. (1989). Searching for alternatives to standardized tests: Whys, whats, and whithers. *Phi Delta Kappan, 70,* 683-687.

Harp, B. (1991). *Assessment and evaluation in whole language programs.* Norwood, MA: Christopher-Gordon.

Johnston, P. (1992). *Constructive evaluation of literate activity.* New York: Longman.

Kemp, M. (1989). *Watching children read and write: Observational records for children with special needs.* Portsmouth, NH: Heinemann.

Maeroff, G. (1991). Assessing alternative assessment. *Phi Delta Kappan, 73,* 272-281.

Neill, D., & Medina, N. (1989). Standardized testing: Harmful to educational health. *Phi Delta Kappan, 70,* 688-697.

Shepard, L. (1989). Why we need better assessments. *Educational Leadership, 46*(7), 4-9.

Tierney, R. J., Carter, M. A., & Desai, L. E. (1991). *Portfolio assessment in the reading-writing classroom.* Norwood, MA: Christopher-Gordon.

Wiggins, G. (1989). A true test: Towards more authentic and equitable assessment. *Phi Delta Kappan, 70,* 703-713.

Winograd, P., & Jones, D. (1992). The use of portfolios in performance assessment. *New Directions in Education Reform, 1,* 37-50.

Winograd, P., Paris, S., & Bridge, C. (1991). Improving the assessment of literacy. *The Reading Teacher, 45,* 108-116.

The Wonder Years. (1991). Frankfort: The Kentucky Department of Education.

THREE

Ensuring Educational Accountability

C. SCOTT TRIMBLE

This chapter deals with the issues of accountability within Kentucky's performance-based student assessment program. It outlines the procedures used in setting performance goals for all schools in the Commonwealth and the rationale behind those procedures. Also discussed are the guidelines for granting rewards to schools that demonstrate exceptional improvement and levying sanctions on schools that fail to show significant progress.

Goals of the Kentucky Reform Act

The Kentucky Education Reform Act (KERA) specifies seven capacities for Kentucky schools. These capacities are translated into six goals.

Understanding these goals is essential to understanding the Kentucky Instructional Results Information System (KIRIS) and the School Assessment and Accountability Program. In essence, the capacities and goals are the basis for all of the strands of Kentucky's reform initiative.

Capacities

The seven capacities set forth in KERA include the following:

1. Communication skills necessary to function in a complex and changing civilization;
2. Knowledge to make economic, social, and political choices;
3. Understanding of governmental processes as they affect the community, the state, and the nation;
4. Sufficient self-knowledge and knowledge of his or her mental and physical wellness;
5. Sufficient grounding in the arts to enable each student to appreciate his or her cultural and historical heritage;
6. Sufficient preparation to choose and pursue his or her life's work intelligently; and
7. Skills to enable him or her to compete favorably with students in other states.

Goals

The six goals derived from these capacities include the following:

1. Schools shall expect a high level of achievement of all students.
2. Schools shall develop their students' ability to
   a. use basic communication and mathematics skills for purposes and situations they will encounter throughout their lives;
   b. apply core concepts and principles from mathematics, the sciences, the arts, the humanities, social studies, and practical-living studies to situations they will encounter throughout their lives;
   c. become self-sufficient individuals;
   d. become responsible members of a family, a work group, or a community, including demonstrating effectiveness in community service;
   e. think and solve problems in school situations and in a variety of situations they will encounter in life;
   f. connect and integrate experiences and new knowledge from all subject matter fields with what they have pre-

viously learned and build on past learning experiences to acquire new information through various media sources.

3. Schools shall increase their students' rate of school attendance.
4. Schools shall reduce their students' dropout and retention rates.
5. Schools shall reduce physical and mental health barriers to learning.
6. Schools shall be measured on the proportion of students who make a successful transition to work, postsecondary education, and the military.

The Statute: Assessment Requirements

The statute required that Kentucky establish an interim assessment, similar to the National Assessment of Educational Progress (NAEP), designed to measure student achievement in reading, math, science, social studies, and writing. It also required that this assessment be administered at Grades 4, 8, and 12, and that it be capable of providing national comparative data. Furthermore, the statute required that a primarily performance-based assessment be established by the 1995-1996 school year. The interim assessment was, therefore, referred to as "transitional." A portion of the statute describing these requirements is included in Appendix A.

Accountability Requirements

The statute also states, "It is the intent of the General Assembly that schools succeed with all students and receive the appropriate consequences in proportion to that success" (Kentucky Revised Statute 158.6455, 1990). This statement set the tone of the entire accountability program. The clear expectation is that schools throughout the Commonwealth steadily increase their percentage of successful students, including that population of students considered to be "at risk of failure."

According to the statute, the school is to be the "basic unit" of accountability. Some measure of accountability also is required at the district level, however, for the purpose of including in the accountability system staff members attached to the central office and not assigned to a school.

The statute further makes the accountability system "high-stakes," based on the computation of an "accountability index" for each school. This is done by establishing a "baseline" score using the results from assessments administered in the spring of the 1991-1992 school year. The Kentucky State Board for Elementary and Secondary Education then establishes a "threshold" for each school that it is expected to meet by the end of the following biennium. This threshold takes into account the difficulty of obtaining large amounts of growth as the index approaches very high levels. Thus the amount of growth required of high-achieving schools is not as much as that expected of low-achieving schools.

If a school exceeds its biennium threshold by 1 percentage point or more, the instructional staff members in that school are to receive a financial reward. A school that reaches its threshold but does not exceed it is considered successful and on track but ineligible for any special rewards.

A school that improves but does not reach its threshold is required to produce a school improvement plan describing how it will meet the threshold in the next biennium. Such a school also is eligible for school improvement funds allocated by the General Assembly. If that school fails to meet its threshold for a second biennium, it receives the additional services of a "Kentucky Distinguished Educator." The Distinguished Educators are specially trained consultants assigned to schools to assist in planning requirements, in the use of school improvement funds, and in other curricular and instructional decisions. If the school fails to meet its threshold a third biennium, it becomes a *school in crisis.*

A school that experiences a decline in its accountability index of 5 percentage points or less is required to produce a school improvement plan describing how it will meet its threshold in the next biennium. Such a school also is eligible for school improvement funds allocated by the General Assembly and receives the additional services of a Kentucky Distinguished Educator. If that school still fails to meet its threshold in the second biennium, it is considered a *school in crisis.*

Finally, there is the case of a school that experiences a decline of *more* than 5 percentage points in its baseline accountability index. This school immediately becomes a *school in crisis.* Some of the consequences of being declared a school in crisis include the requirement to develop a school improvement plan and the assignment of a Kentucky Distinguished Educator. In this case, however, the Distinguished Educator must evaluate the staff at the school within 6 months and determine the disposition of all full- and part-time certified staff members, including such options as continued employment, transfer to another site, or dismissal. The principal of the affected school must notify all parents of students in the school of its classification and of their right to transfer their child to a school that is not considered "in crisis." Although the school is designated as the base unit of accountability, an equivalent high-stakes accountability requirement applies to staff members who are attached to the district central office.

A summary of the various aspects of the accountability structure is presented in Figure 3.1. Consequences are viewed in this figure over the first three accountability cycles or bienniums.

Inclusion of All Students

The statute states that *all* students, including those who are considered at risk of failure, must be included in the accountability system. This includes students who are transitory and may be in the school for a relatively short period of time. To clarify this point, the decision was made to have schools be accountable for all students enrolled on the 20th day of instruction. It is assumed that all students will be enrolled in some school on that day.

At-risk populations include students with disabilities. These students are to be included in the accountability system in one of two ways. Students with disabilities may participate in the assessments using those adaptations that are consistent with the normal instructional process and that are documented in the student's Individual Education Plan (IEP) or 504 Plan (T. C. Boysen, personal communication, February 9, 1993). If a student's disability

A School's Accountability Index	1994	1996	1998
Exceeds its threshold by 1 point or more	Reward	Reward	Reward
Is greater than or equal to threshold and less than 1 point more than threshold	Declared successful	Declared successful	Declared successful
Is greater than or equal to baseline and is less than threshold	Plan, funds	Plan, funds, and Distinguished Educator	Plan, funds, and Distinguished Educator Crisis
Is less than baseline and is greater than 5 points below baseline	Plan, funds, and Distinguished Educator	Crisis	Crisis
Is less than or equal to 5 points below baseline	Crisis	Crisis	Crisis

Figure 3.1. Various Aspects of the Accountability Structure

prevents participation in the regular curriculum with all assistance and adaptive devices made available, that student must participate through an alternate portfolio process. This exception, however, is expected to affect only between 1% and 2% of the total population of schoolchildren in the Commonwealth.

Description of KIRIS Components

The KIRIS assessment design includes two major measurement components: a *cognitive* component designed to address Goal 2 of the reform act and a *noncognitive* component designed to address Goals 3, 4, and 6. The major portion of the accountability index is based on Goal 2, which is the cognitive component. The noncognitive component related to Goals 3, 4, and 6 deals with the measurement of attendance rates, retention rates, dropout rates, and successful transition to adult life. Goals 1 and 5 are dealt with at a philosophical level.

The requirement that schools expect a high level of achievement for all students is addressed in the achievement standards that are associated with the cognitive measures. At an early phase in the assessment development, the decision was made to consider achievement in terms of "standards of achievement," as opposed to normative comparisons or other more traditional approaches to reporting achievement.

The requirement to reduce physical and mental barriers to learning is to be considered within the total school accountability system. It may be, for example, that the reason a school did not meet its required level of growth is that physical and mental barriers to learning were not reduced. Therefore, all school improvement plans are required to include a review of possible barriers to learning, with appropriate strategies to address these barriers.

Goal 2: The Cognitive Component

Most of the work that has gone into developing the assessment program has been devoted to designing and implementing the cognitive component. The statute provided a 5-year window within which the assessment system was to evolve into a primarily performance-based assessment program. The design of the program includes three types of assessment that shift in overall importance through that 5-year period. These three types of assessment include the following:

1. The KIRIS transitional tests
2. The KIRIS performance events
3. The KIRIS portfolio assessment

In the early phases of implementation, the transitional tests weigh most heavily in the calculation of the accountability index. In later phases, however, the performance events and the portfolio assessments are emphasized, with the major focus being on the portfolios.

Transitional Tests

The KIRIS transitional tests cover the content areas of reading, math, science, and social studies and consist of two types of items: multiple-choice and constructed-response items. For each content area, the tests for 4th-, 8th-, and 12th-grade students each include a set of 40 common multiple-choice items. Also included are 180 matrix-sampled, multiple-choice items administered in sets of 15 across 12 forms of the tests. Each test, therefore, contains a total of 55 multiple-choice items. A set of three constructed-response items also is included in the tests in the four content areas, as well as a set of 12 matrix-sampled, constructed-response items, one in each of the 12 forms of the tests.

Writing in the transitional tests is measured through nine pairs of prompts, administered in a matrix-sample design, from which the student selects one. Students are given 90 minutes to write to the selected prompt.

The tests for each of the five content areas are designed to be administered in 90 minutes, although students are allowed an additional 45 minutes to finish, if needed. Each test can therefore take up to 2 hours and 15 minutes to administer. The intent is to allow all students adequate time to complete the tests.

The transitional tests are viewed as "transitional" in two major ways. First, they provide the means for moving away from a statewide assessment system based on traditional multiple-choice, norm-referenced tests, toward one that is based on more authentic, performance-based assessments. Second, they provide a link to more traditional measurement technology while the technology of performance-based assessment is being developed and refined. The transitional tests are also being used to meet some of the more traditional assessment needs of Chapter 1 evaluation and to link results to NAEP reading, math, and writing scores for the purpose of providing national comparative data.

It should be noted that when development of the assessment program began, the role of the multiple-choice and constructed-response items was not clearly defined. After the first administration of the transitional tests, it was discovered that the reliability of the constructed-response items at the school level compared favorably with that of the multiple-choice items. Because of the focus on school-level results for accountability purposes, it was possible then to place all accountability requirements on the constructed-response items.

This decision was viewed as being consistent with Kentucky's requirement to move in the direction of a primarily performance-based assessment program. It also provided strong direction to those concerned with instructional processes. One purpose of moving to performance-based assessments was to provide incentives for instructional activities to be less oriented to a basic skills mode of operation but to be more oriented to an analytic, problem-solving mode of operation.

As the transitional tests are refined, interdisciplinary items will be embedded among the matrix-sampled pool of constructed-response items. These items will combine the arts and humanities and the concepts of practical-living or vocational studies with reading, math, science, and social studies concepts. Each student will be asked to respond to five common and two matrix-sampled constructed-response items across 12 forms. As a result, there will be a total of 29 items in each content area except writing, where students continue to respond to one of a pair of writing prompts.

Performance Events

The performance events have been referred to as "on demand" performance assessments. In the initial assessments, four events each were administered in the content areas of math, science, and social studies. In subsequent assessments certain of these events were made interdisciplinary (e.g., science/math, math/social studies). In addition, arts and humanities, and practical-living or vocational-studies events were added.

Performance events represent a critical feature of the assessment program in that they focus attention on two important aspects of the reform. The first is that they compel instruction to focus on the application of skills in order to produce products that can be evaluated. Second, they require students to work together in teams to find solutions to problems. The performance events are currently formulated such that students first are asked to do certain tasks as a group. Based on that experience, each student then produces a written product. For example, a group of four students may be asked to observe and record data measuring the distance balls made of different materials bounce when dropped from a specified height. Based on their observations, the group may be asked to produce certain data tables or other individual products. From this information, each student then may be asked to answer questions that would be dependent on how well the group worked together to make observations and to record data.

Portfolio Assessments

The portfolio assessments represent the vision of KIRIS and the School Accountability Program. In an ideal assessment program, data would be gathered within the instructional process; evidence about the achievement of students would be compiled in a portfolio; this evidence would be evaluated and judged in a standard way; and school, district, and statewide data would be compiled from the process. Under KIRIS, portfolios are not restricted to a paper folder, as is often perceived. Rather, it could include, but is certainly not limited to, devices such as videotapes, computer storage mediums, or other similar devices.

Ideally in a portfolio assessment, the instruction and the assessment are one and the same. Portfolio assessments basically gather data from the daily activities of students and teachers. This feature must be emphasized to prevent the portfolio from becoming an added assessment burden placed on classroom teachers. It also is important if teachers are to become a meaningful part of the decision about how effective schools are.

In the initial implementation of the portfolio assessment, only a writing portfolio was included, consisting of six to seven of a student's "best works." The portfolios were to be developed over the first 7 months of the school year and then were evaluated by the classroom teacher. Each classroom teacher took part in 6 to 8 hours of training on portfolio development and scoring over the school year. This training was conducted through a pyramid structure with state and contractor trainers at the top, filtering down through writing cluster leaders and classroom teachers. In the second year of implementation, math portfolios were phased in, as well as "alternate portfolios," for the purpose of including in the assessment and accountability program those students with moderate to severe disabilities.

Reporting Cognitive Data in Standards

Early in the development process, it was decided that student data should be reported in terms of standards that could be clearly understood and would clearly communicate what students have accomplished. After some consideration, the performance categories of Novice, Apprentice, Proficient, and Distinguished were designated. These names are not as important as their definition and the student products that are accepted as evidence of the attainment of a particular standard.

The first goal of KERA focuses on the expectation of high levels of performance from each and every child in the Commonwealth. This goal guided the standard-setting process, which began by first defining the "Proficient" standard.

Proficient is considered the level of performance that will allow the student to be competitive in the economic and social environment of the next century. The performance expectations for this level are, therefore, designed to be high. Because this performance standard is thought to represent a major increase in the performance level of most students currently enrolled in Kentucky schools, other standards also were defined.

Novice is the standard of students who can demonstrate little or none of the qualities related to the Proficient standard.

Apprentice is considered an intermediate level between Novice and Proficient. At this level, students are presenting tangible evidence of "making progress" toward the Proficient standard.

Distinguished is the standard that was established to recognize the accomplishments of that small percentage of students who exceed even the Proficient standard.

A more detailed description of the KIRIS standards and their interpretation is available in the *KIRIS Technical Report* (1991-1992), which may be obtained from Advanced Systems in Measurement and Evaluation, Inc., Dover, New Hampshire.

Goals 3, 4, and 6: The Noncognitive Indicators

The noncognitive indicators refer to the statutory requirement for schools to (a) increase attendance rates, (b) decrease dropout rates, (c) decrease retention rates (failure to promote in grade level), and to (d) increase the percentage of students making a successful transition to adult life. In this regard, the law defines successful transition to adult life as having successfully entered the workforce, having become a homemaker, having entered post-secondary education, or having entered the military.

Although the noncognitive indicators make up less than 16% of the accountability index, they have received serious scrutiny by local and state interests. Of particular concern are both definitional issues and data collection procedures.

Percentage in attendance has remained constant in both definition and data collection for many years in the Commonwealth. This is because attendance data are an important factor in school-funding procedures. Retention rates have been revised, however, mainly to accommodate changes brought about by the primary education strand of KERA, which replaces what were traditionally Grades K, 1, 2, and 3, with an ungraded primary program. Within this program, "failure to promote" is no longer considered to be a feature or statistic. That is, students are to remain in the primary program until they are ready to enter the 4th grade and progress normally. Retention rates, therefore, now include only grades 4 through 12, as opposed to Grades K through 12, as was previously the case. In addition, schools have the opportunity to consider the impact of summer school programs on retention rates, so it is not necessary to collect these data until the fall of the year.

Dropout rates have been redefined to be consistent with the definition by the National Center for Education Statistics (NCES), in which summer dropouts and unverified transfers to other schools are counted as dropouts. Students whose reentry can be verified,

however, are not counted as dropouts. These data also are collected in the fall.

Although the transition to the "adult life" factor is defined to
be consistent with definitions used previously in Kentucky, there
was a need to improve the method of data collection. In essence,
NCES verification procedures for determining the status of potential dropouts was adapted for use in determining the status of
graduates. To meet the January 1st deadline for informing schools
of their accountability index score, the timeframe for gathering
these transition data was restricted to the period between Septem-
ber 1 and November 15.

Local School and District Accountability

The statute makes clear that the school is to be the basic unit of
accountability. Nevertheless, a district-level accountability index
was also deemed necessary for individuals and services provided
from the district central office. This index was designed to be
simple and easily reproduced by staff members being held accountable and by the general public. In essence, it is a simple
combination of the data from the elements of the assessment
described above for each school.

At the school level, the constructed-response items of the
KIRIS transitional tests yield two estimates of the percentage of
students who score in each of the four standard categories (Novice,
Apprentice, Proficient, and Distinguished) in the content areas of
reading, math, science, and social studies. One estimate comes
from the three commonly administered items in each content area,
and the second comes from the 12 matrix-sampled items. The
administration of the performance events yields estimates of the
percentage of students achieving each standard in math, science,
and social studies. The writing and mathematics portfolios result
in similar estimates. These distributions of students within these
standard categories, along with the percentage in attendance,
retention rates, dropout rates, and the percentage of graduates
making a successful transition to adult life, are combined to form
the accountability index.

The procedure used to combine the percentages of students
scoring in various standard categories was simply to assign weights

Table 3.1. Weights Assigned to Performance Standard
Categories

Category	Relative Value
Novice	0.0
Apprentice	0.4
Proficient	1.0
Distinguished	1.4

to each of the categories. Because the statute consistently referred to a percentage scale in discussions of the current level or increase in the level of successful students, a value of 100 was set for the goal of all students scoring at the Proficient level. With this in mind, a value of 0 was assigned to the Novice level, which was considered to be the definable minimum. A value of 2 was assigned to the Apprentice level, 5 to the Proficient level, and 7 to the Distinguished level. These weights combine to form the percentage scale (5 converts to 1.00 or 100%) illustrated in Table 3.1.

To produce the contribution of each component of the assessment, weights are multiplied by the percentage of students who score within each standard category. A detailed description of this process is included in Appendix B. The worksheet included in this description was distributed to every school district in the Commonwealth, with the strong encouragement to share the materials with all staff members, especially school principals.

Table 3.2 summarizes the contribution of each component of the assessment with regard to the five content areas: reading, math, science, social studies, and writing. These apply to the computation of the accountability baseline for Grades 4, 8, and 12. Because the application of the four noncognitive factors differs depending on grade level, their contribution is summarized separately in Table 3.3.

The relative contribution of the noncognitive factors reflects a combination of value judgments and data availability. Transition to adult life is thought to be a very important factor, but the collection of such data at the fourth- and eighth-grade levels makes no sense. Thus, although important, the inclusion of the dropout factor is not definable below the seventh-grade level. At

Table 3.2. Summary of the Contribution of Each Content Area for Grades 4, 8, and 12 (in percentages)

Component	Reading	Math	Science	Social Studies	Writing
Transitional tests					
Common	50	40	40	40	0
Matrix	50	40	40	40	0
Performance events	0	20	20	20	0
Portfolios	0	0	0	0	100

Table 3.3. Summary of the Contribution of Noncognitive Factors to the Accountability Index for Grades 4, 8, and 12 (in percentages)

Component	Grade 4	Grade 8	Grade 12
Attendance rates	80	40	20.0
Retention rates	20	40	5.0
Dropout rates	0	20	37.5
Transition to adult life	0	0	37.5

the middle school level, on the other hand, retention rates are of far greater importance. At the elementary level, only attendance and retention rates are clearly definable. And because of the implementation of the nongraded primary program, only data at the fourth- and fifth-grade levels will be used in determining this factor in most schools.

Producing the Accountability Baseline Index

The calculation of the accountability baseline index is summarized briefly here, but described in detail in Appendix B. Recall, an accountability index score of 100 represents having brought all of the students to a Proficient level of performance and reaching perfection on the noncognitive factors: 100% attendance, 0% dropouts, and so on. To establish the accountability baseline for a school, the five cognitive factors and one noncognitive factor were simply averaged. A summary of the statewide data from the baseline computations is included in Appendix C.

As can be seem from these data, only about 10% to 15% of Kentucky's students were at the desired level when the assessment program was begun. Progress from this baseline is then charted for the next 20 years. In this way, KERA is not viewed as an "immediate fix," but rather as a process by which valuable goals can be obtained over a reasonable time period. The accountability index scale currently is a compensatory scale, in that high performance in one content area can compensate for low performance in another. Likewise, having more students score at the Distinguished level can compensate for students scoring below the Proficient level. Over time, however, as schools are pressed to meet established accountability threshold requirements, the compensatory nature of the scale will be drastically reduced.

Producing the Accountability Threshold—Expected Improvement and Growth

The accountability threshold is that accountability index value a school is expected (and required) to attain when results from the next 2 years of assessments are combined. Because KIRIS is conducted each year but accountability indexes calculated each biennium, the threshold is determined by calculating one tenth of the growth needed by a school to reach an accountability index score of 100 after 20 years. Thus the accountability index might be considered a "growth index." It has been stipulated, however, that a school's current accountability index score cannot be based on data from expanded portions of the assessment system. For example, when the performance events and portfolios are expanded, these will not be included in the calculation of a school's current accountability index. They will be included, however, in determining subsequent accountability thresholds. In this manner, the assessment and accountability system will expand over time in

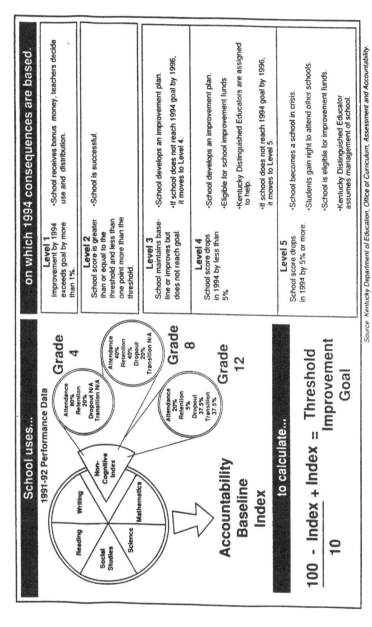

Figure 3.2 Kentucky School Performance Accountability System

Source: Kentucky Department of Education, Office of Curriculum, Assessment and Accountability.

both its content and the types of assessment included. The calculation of the accountability index and the consequences of accountability decisions are summarized in Figure 3.2.

Conclusion

Combining high expectations and reasonable demands in an assessment and accountability program has proven challenging to Kentucky policy makers. The kinds of assessments currently being used in Kentucky have been tried in varying places, but never have they been applied under the pressures of a high-stakes accountability system. It is difficult to determine precisely what amount of growth is reasonable in settings that are drastically different, as is true in schools across the Commonwealth. Therefore, growth expectations are reviewed by the State Board for Elementary and Secondary Education after each assessment cycle. Still, the expectation is clear that, in time, all students and all schools can be successful. All schools in the Commonwealth, regardless of the student population they serve, are expected to obtain an accountability index score of 100 at some time within the next 20 years. The distance between a school's baseline index and 100 is currently considered the "gap," or the total needed improvement. If this gap can be reduced by 10% each biennium, that school will reach an accountability index value of 100 in 20 years. Although certainly challenging, most educators in the Commonwealth are committed to accomplishing that goal.

Reference

Kentucky Instructional Results Information System 1991-1992 Technical Report. Dover, NH: Advanced Systems in Measurement and Evaluation, Inc.

FOUR

A School District's Perspective

BEN R. OLDHAM

Background

As described in earlier chapters, the reform movement in Kentucky began with a lawsuit. Funding for public schools, other educational programs, and humanities programs in the Commonwealth was increased from $1.63 billion to $2.02 billion for 1990-1991, a 22% increase (Luttrell, 1990). Along with increased funding came the more sweeping Kentucky Education Reform Act (KERA), which mandated changes in a variety of areas. The impact of these changes was to be evaluated by what is perhaps the most significant change of all: an assessment program based on the actual performance of Kentucky's public school students.

Impact on a Local School District

The Kentucky Instructional Results Information System (KIRIS) is the assessment mechanism designed to measure the accomplishments of Kentucky public schools in meeting the goals of KERA. Clearly, the program is taken seriously by school-based persons as well as community members because results are likely to be presented as an indication of school quality. Furthermore, because the assessment program is high-stakes by design, significant attention undoubtedly will be devoted to improving results, regardless of the impact on "real" achievement.

Impact on Individual Students

The greatest benefit to students from KIRIS could be its impact on the procedures that teachers use to establish expectations for student learning. The law states, "It is the intent of the General Assembly that schools succeed with all students and receive appropriate consequences to that success" (Kentucky Revised Statute 158.6455, 1992). In other words, schools can no longer use socioeconomic status, ethnicity, or home environment as excuses for low levels of student performance. Instead, they must bring to bear whatever resources are at their disposal to ensure that all students in their charge learn well.

This statement of law supports an outcome-based education philosophy and dramatically departs from a traditional bell curve orientation. It compels educators at the local level to change their way of thinking about the potential of all students to achieve and to reach high levels of learning (Guskey, 1992). Specifically, it presses them to base classroom assessment on what students know and are able to do, rather than on relative standing among classmates. The traditional textbook-driven curriculum must be replaced by one that is based on identified learner outcomes. Curriculum tracking must be reduced, and the instructional materials and methods used in programs for gifted students must be made accessible to all students.

Under KIRIS, individual student results are reported for both portfolios and the transitional tests. As described earlier, the transitional tests are made up of multiple-choice and open-response items. To gain a broader sampling of the curriculum, matrix-sampled items are included in the reading, mathematics, science, and social studies subtests. These matrix-sampled items are used in calculating school results, but only common items are included in determining the scores of individual students.

Based on their performance, students are classified in one of four performance categories: Novice, Apprentice, Proficient, or Distinguished. Students' classifications are determined only by their scores on the three common open-response items included in each subtest. Thus, although matrix sampling provides a sufficient item pool for acceptable reliability at the school level, reliability is not adequate to permit accurate decisions about individual students (Kentucky Department of Education, 1992).

For schools, this lack of reliability presents several problems. Many programmatic decisions made at the school level require reliable information on individual students. Academic program placement decisions, for example, are made as students proceed from elementary school to middle school, and from middle school to high school. Schools typically use scores from standardized achievement measures as a valuable piece of information in making these placement decisions. Because of the amount of time and budget dollars devoted to the performance assessment program, it will be impossible for schools to devote additional time and financial resources to these standardized measures. As a result, placement decisions will have to be made on the basis of less reliable and much more limited information.

In addition, many special programs operating within schools require standardized achievement data for admission or evaluation purposes. Programs for the academically gifted and talented, Chapter 1, and the Duke Talent Search Project are but a few examples of programs that historically have required the use of standardized, norm-referenced tests. Although elimination of such norm-referenced tests for selection and evaluation may be desirable, other reliable information must be available to fulfill program requirements.

Parents and other community members also have become accustomed to interpreting test information from a normative perspective. When the performance assessment results are presented to them, they continue to ask, "Yes, but how does my child stack up nationally?" And when national comparisons are not offered, the charge is sometimes made that the schools are hiding something. Educating parents to the intricacies of criterion-referenced, performance assessments is a monumental task. Although parents typically offer no major objection to the performance assessments, they do seem unwilling to give up some reliance on normative comparisons.

School-based educators in Kentucky are also concerned about a high-stakes assessment program that could result in sanctions being imposed on a school, with no component for student accountability. Because results are unreliable at the individual student level, they cannot be used as an incentive to motivate students to expend their greatest efforts. As a result, scores mean everything to the school but nothing to students. This concern is especially evident at the senior high school level, where high school students are involved in the high-stakes school assessment during the second semester of their senior year. It is possible for real improvements in student performance to occur and yet go undetected, because the assessment program is high-stakes for schools but no-stakes for students.

Some schools in Kentucky have tried to counter this problem by establishing performance requirements for students. These performance requirements stipulate that students must submit a portfolio of their work in order to graduate from high school. Some have gone so far as to require a specified level of performance on the portfolio. Requirements such as these will place some of the onus on students and, it is hoped, will make them more effective participants in the high-stakes assessment process.

Impact on Instruction

In many Kentucky school districts, children have been required to take norm-referenced achievement tests in designated grades for at least the last 15 years. Results from these multiple-choice tests are considered by many to be an indication of the quality of a school's instructional program. Skill-based item analysis reports provided by the test publishers are used to diagnose areas of weakness and to prescribe needed changes in a school's curriculum. Unfortunately, the importance attached to these tests also has led to an overemphasis on teaching children specific test-taking strategies designed to improve their performance on multiple-choice items.

Because KIRIS is primarily performance based, preparation activities now differ markedly. The hope of the designers of KIRIS is that classroom activities consistently reflect the more authentic assessment formats. As a result, adapting instruction to the required assessments is seen as a positive development, rather than as a detraction from valued learning. Such adaptations in instructional procedures are unlikely to occur, however, without substantial professional development.

As described earlier, to estimate a school's performance in an authentic setting, students in grades 4, 8, and 12 are brought into a room, usually the school library, where they respond to 1 of 12 performance events. Students are randomly assigned to events and work in small groups for approximately 20 minutes. The proctor then interrupts the group work and directs students to prepare an individual response to the task.

Of the 12 events that a student may be asked to complete, only 4 come from the subject areas of mathematics, science, and social studies. Because a student encounters only 1 event, and because there are only small numbers of students per event, reliability is greatly limited. This is true regardless of the quality of the performance events or the interrater consistency in scoring. External validity is also problematic, for it seems unlikely that results from only 4 performance events accurately represent school-level achievement in mathematics, science, or social studies.

Many school-based educators in Kentucky expected the performance-based assessment activities to be a driving force in the reform movement. Because of the lack of measurement reliability in the performance events (see Kentucky Department of Education, 1992), its contribution to the accountability index has been limited to only about 10%. Noting this, teachers have made relatively few changes in their teaching practices and, as a result, the use of performance events has had relatively little impact on instruction.

As mentioned earlier, one of the primary goals of KERA is the communication of knowledge in reading, mathematics, science, and social studies. Many teachers are concerned, however, that, although the communication of knowledge is important, the direct assessment of knowledge is not given sufficient consideration. Items that assess writing in response to reading, mathematics, science, and social studies comprise approximately 57% of the accountability index. With the inclusion of portfolio scores, the writing component of the accountability index makes up approximately 74% of the total score. Although most teachers support the importance of written communication, many believe that explicit knowledge of a subject in and of itself is inadequately represented. Mathematics and science teachers in particular are concerned about the extensive amount of instructional time being allocated to writing.

Assessment Across Subject Domains

To the credit of the Kentucky Department of Education and the assessment contractor, Advanced Systems, Inc., local school district personnel have been heavily involved in the development and review of test items, performance events, and the establishment of scoring standards. The decision rule to classify students as Novice, Apprentice, Proficient, or Distinguished, for example, was developed by subject area specialists from Kentucky schools under the direction of the professionals from Advanced Systems, Inc. Although this classification process is good, the scoring rules for each subtest were developed independently. Therefore, the distribution of students across achievement categories for different subject areas is not linked. This, in turn, leads to interpretation problems at the school level. If results show, for example, different distributions of achievement in reading, mathematics, science, and social studies, it is uncertain whether these represent real differences in academic performance, or whether they are simply the result of higher or lower standards being applied to the student performance in those areas. It is also possible for the professionals who develop the scoring rules to establish more challenging standards in one particular subject in order to get schools to devote additional attention to that area.

Teacher Involvement and Workload

Teachers and other school-based educators are generally supportive of a program that assesses what students know and are able to do. There is concern, however, that many of the required activities do not directly support improved instructional practice. For example, KERA requires that schools verify the postgraduation status of former students. This verification can come from a variety of sources. Nevertheless, most of the time, these data are collected through telephone calls to the student or to the student's parents, which is a very time-consuming task.

Another time-consuming responsibility requires secondary schools to verify the status of students who have withdrawn from the school. In many cases this verification requires only a request for students' records from another school. Oftentimes, however, students relocate during the summer months and enroll in a different school in the fall. When this occurs, the sending school must spend time verifying these students' enrollment status, and the receiving school must spend time trying to locate the records. No one denies the importance of locating all students and placing them in programs that lead to a high school diploma. Still, these additional responsibilities are placed on schools without commensurate increases in personnel to perform such tasks.

The multiple scoring of portfolios in writing and mathematics in Grades 4, 8, and 12 increases the workload for teachers as well. Most teachers understand that portfolios must become a part of the classroom assessment process. But the need for interrater reliability requires all teachers to assign the same or nearly the same score when they rate a portfolio. To check and improve rating consistency, a sample of portfolios from each teacher must be rescored by another teacher. If the scores are found to be discrepant, the first teacher must rescore all portfolios in the class. Besides the embarrassment this is likely to cause, it requires a great deal of additional time from all of the teachers involved. This is especially problematic in Grade 4 where a single teacher must maintain and evaluate multiple portfolios for each student—one in writing and one for mathematics.

Growth in Achievement

KERA is based on the premise that all students can learn and achieve at a high level. The assessment design, therefore, establishes a common achievement goal that all schools in the Commonwealth are expected to reach by the end of a 20-year period.

Because the starting achievement point for each school is different, but the ultimate goal is the same for all, schools must realize different achievement gains as they progress. A high-achieving school is required to make smaller annual achievement gains to reach its goal than is a low-achieving school. As a result, schools that serve the most disadvantaged communities face the greatest challenge in overcoming barriers to learning. These schools must exceed the educational growth of more advantaged schools and must do so without substantial increases in support.

Influence on Staff Development

In an assessment-driven reform effort such as KERA, it is expected that what is measured and the methodology used in measuring will influence what is taught and how it is taught (Popham, 1987). This is magnified in KERA because KIRIS represents a high-stakes assessment. Preparing teachers for a performance-based assessment program by providing staff development activities that are directly related to the assessments could be a highly beneficial outcome of the reform act.

It is essential, therefore, that staff development activities be designed to improve students' abilities to communicate their knowledge in all curriculum areas. Teachers must be retrained to teach writing in response to mathematics, science, and social studies. They also must be taught how to elicit higher order thinking behaviors and how to develop assessment tasks moving from using verbs such as "list," "define," and "identify," to verbs such as "explain," "compare and contrast," and "defend."

Because the performance events included in KIRIS require students to work in groups to solve authentic problems, simply offering lecture presentations of material is no longer appropriate. To optimize student performance, teachers must alter their teaching practices to make them more consistent with the assessments. This will require extensive retraining for many classroom teachers, especially for those who teach at the secondary level where lecture methods are so prevalent.

The need to respond to the numerous legislated mandates associated with KERA has led most school districts in the Commonwealth to focus on procedures that will cost very little, yet will have a significant impact on assessment results. In other words, they have sought a "quick fix." Although strategies such as these may work in the first biennium assessment, it is unlikely their effects will endure. Long-term professional development programs designed to increase the pedagogic skills of all teachers must be provided.

Conclusion

Only time will tell if the mandates of the Kentucky Educational Reform Act will result in better educated students leaving public schools throughout the Commonwealth. At the present time we can only speculate and hope. Current evidence indicates, however, that classroom practice has changed little in recent years, despite the fact that our knowledge of the teaching and learning process has increased dramatically. A striking gap remains between what has been shown to work and what is being implemented at the classroom level. If the implementation problems described here can be resolved, a high-stakes, performance-based assessment program such as KIRIS may, indeed, have a positive impact. Compared to testing programs in the past, it seems to be a step in the right direction.

References

Guskey, T. R. (1992). The importance of focusing on student outcomes. *NCA Quarterly, 66*(3), 507-512.

Kentucky Department of Education. (1992). *Kentucky Instructional Results Information System: 1991-92 technical report.* Frankfort: Author.

Luttrell, W. (1990). Education reform in Kentucky: The funding. *School Governance & Administration Exchange, 9,* 1-3.

Popham, W. J. (1987). The merits of measurement-driven instruction. *Phi Delta Kappan, 68,* 679-682.

FIVE

Theoretical and Practical Implications

EDWARD H. HAERTEL

Measurement-driven educational reform has a long and often unhappy history (Glass, 1978; Haertel, 1989; Madaus, 1985). Time and again, legislators have responded to public concerns over the quality of education or the poor skills of graduates by mandating tough new tests of one kind or another, with harsh penalties for the individuals who fail to pass or for the schools that have failed to teach them. Time and again, test scores have risen, public concerns have subsided for a time, and then it has been found that, apart from scores on the tests themselves, there is little or no evidence of any educational improvement.

To be sure, proponents of high-stakes testing can point to some successes. The International Baccalaureate (Freeman, 1987; Godsey, 1989), the New York Regents examinations (Ambach, 1984), and the College Entrance Examination Board's Advanced Placement tests (e.g., Dickey, 1986; Herr, 1991; Whelan, 1989) are often cited as positive examples of sound, rigorous instruction designed around an examination-driven syllabus. All in all, the effects of college entrance examinations on the nation's curricula have probably been salutary (Valentine, 1987). But the good examples cited are mostly of elite, voluntary programs for advantaged students. In most cases, high-stakes testing has failed to bring hope for improvements in achievement (in spite of rising test scores) and has instead resulted in a narrowing of the curriculum to just the knowledge and skills required for the examination, rehearsed in just the form it is required to be demonstrated (Madaus, 1988).

Contemporary advocates of measurement-driven reform denigrate multiple-choice and other objective paper-and-pencil tests, arguing that past failures of high-stakes testing are just what should have been expected with such dreadful instruments. What many of these tests appear to measure is superficial familiarity with innumerable isolated facts. No wonder instruction aimed at improving multiple-choice test scores seems to crowd out group work, class discussions, opportunities for extended writing, and higher order thinking. New forms of authentic, performance-based assessments, the argument goes, will at last usher in the days of tests we really want teachers to teach (Resnick & Resnick, 1992; Wiggins, 1992; Wolf, Bixby, Glenn, & Gardner, 1991; Wolf, LeMahieu, & Eresh, 1992). Although most measurement experts acknowledge that high-stakes multiple-choice tests may encourage low-level, superficial coverage of content at the expense of more valuable instructional activities (Darling-Hammond, 1991), they remain skeptical about the high expectations for high-stakes performance testing (Jaeger, 1991; Koretz, Madaus, Haertel, & Beaton, 1992; Linn, 1993). They also express concern about the substantial technical challenges these new forms of assessment pose (Dunbar, Koretz, & Hoover, 1991; Koretz et al., 1992; Linn, 1993; Shavelson, Baxter, & Pine, 1992; Shepard, 1991).

What does all this say about the Commonwealth of Kentucky's bold experiment? Will it succeed in raising standards and achievement for all segments of the student population? Even if it falls short of the most optimistic predictions, will its net effects be positive? Will they be large enough to justify the accountability program's costs? I see several reasons for cautious optimism. In the remainder of this chapter, I first highlight several important features of the Kentucky Instructional Results Information System (KIRIS) that set it apart from most of the less successful measurement-driven reform initiatives of the past. I then briefly describe some technical issues that will need to be addressed as the program evolves.

Distinctive Strengths of KIRIS

The Kentucky Educational Reform Act (KERA) was passed in response to a court order and a perceived crisis in the quality of public education. KIRIS was born out of frustration with an incremental approach to reform that never seemed to change the status quo. The intent was to shock the system, to make a radical break with educational business as usual, and to set a new course. However, the legislature soberly recognized that new tests alone would not be enough and embedded KIRIS in a comprehensive reform package. As noted in chapter 4, educational funding was increased dramatically to pay for additional teacher training, new educational materials, and other needed changes. In addition, the legislature deserves credit for recognizing that change will take time. Many promising educational innovations have been undermined by an insistence on quick results. KIRIS features a reasonable, phased implementation and a realistic 20-year time line for attaining its ultimate goals. Along the same lines, the Kentucky reforms take account of the different starting points of various schools, differentiating improvement targets according to initial achievement levels.

Turning from the legislative mandate to the KIRIS design and implementation, there are other positive features. In subtle ways, high-stakes testing can shift responsibility for failure from the educational system to the students who fail to make the grade (Cohen & Haney, 1980). Although students must be shown that hard work pays off and that their choices bear real consequences, they must not be made the scapegoats for having received a poor education. As Scott Trimble explains in chapter 3, in Kentucky the consequences of failure are borne by the schools, not the students. At least for the next several years, this seems appropriate. However, KIRIS may not yet have struck quite the right balance between holding students blameless for shortcomings of the system and holding them responsible for their own actions. As Ben Oldham notes in chapter 4, when students, especially in the upper grades, are asked to sit for examinations that bear no personal consequences, they may not exert maximum effort, regardless of the consequences for their schools.

Teachers, like students, must be apportioned appropriate but not excessive responsibility for testing outcomes. The rhetoric of some recent testing reforms has put too much blame on teachers, suggesting that if they just worked harder (perhaps talked faster?) results would improve. In contrast to this position, a positive feature of the Kentucky reforms, vital to their success, is the respect accorded teachers. If a school is found to be in crisis, the work of each individual teacher will be closely examined, and transfers or dismissals are possible, but even then there are numerous procedural safeguards. Short of such catastrophic failure, teachers are seen as the key to the solution, not the problem. As is clear especially from Winograd and Webb's discussion in chapter 2, teachers are regarded as professionals and as collaborators in reform. Numerous training opportunities are being provided to help them update their skills, and their direct participation in creating new reporting formats and instructional materials will go a long way toward assuring that by and large they work with the new system and not against it.

Again, a word of caution. As Ben Oldham notes in chapter 4, scoring and sometimes rescoring portfolios may add significantly to teachers' workloads. Additional training takes time, and so does redesigning instruction. In the short run, creating curriculum-embedded assessments and scoring portfolios can be a stimulating collegial experience and a powerful form of in-service education. Over time, however, as the work becomes more routine, those benefits will diminish. Moreover, the scoring burden will increase as transitional tests are phased out and the system moves toward heavier reliance on performance-based assessments. The increased workload for teachers must be acknowledged if their good will is to be maintained.

Another strength of the KIRIS reform is its inclusiveness. In most high-stakes assessments, ways are found to exclude students with learning disabilities, limited English proficiency, or who for other reasons may fare poorly. At the high school level, high-stakes testing programs may drive weak students out of the educational system altogether (McDill, Natriello, & Pallas, 1985). In Kentucky, as Scott Trimble states in chapter 3, a commitment to the inclusion of *all* students sets the tone for the entire accountability program. Reasonable provisions are made for alternative assessments of students with special needs, but no one is to be abandoned or excluded. If procedural safeguards to keep track of all students are implemented responsibly, groups of students that may bring down schools' average scores should be well protected and well served. Keeping track of students who "disappear" and monitoring "successful transition to adult life" may be onerous to school administrators, but these are important safeguards. Continued vigilance will be required to assure that they remain effective.

Even if all students remain in the system, there may still be adverse consequences for those thought likely to score poorly. Weak students may be retained an extra year in the 3rd, 7th, or 11th grades, for example, to improve their scores on the high-stakes examinations at Grades 4, 8, or 12. At the 7th and 11th grades, excessive retentions will be noted and will count against the school. The ungraded K-3 primary program, however, combined with a high-stakes test in Grade 4, may encourage inappropriate retention of children who would be better served by the 4th-grade curriculum. Other, less obvious responses of schools should also be monitored. Principals may respond to KIRIS by putting their best teachers at critical grade levels. Resources may be shifted from gifted and talented programs to those students at greater risk of failure. Such changes are not necessarily bad, but they merit consideration as potential unintended consequences of the accountability program.

Perhaps the most important strength of KIRIS is the quality and comprehensiveness of the assessments themselves. The tests used take a variety of different forms and pose engaging and challenging tasks for children. Rather than pretending that the high-stakes test is just a "core" and that teachers will supplement instruction on tested skills with additional material, the system aims eventually to assess virtually all of the 75 learner outcomes described in earlier chapters. Even more significant, KIRIS respects and maintains the distinction between assessment for accountability and assessment for instruction (e.g., Cole, 1988). As Peter Winograd and Karen Schuster Webb explain in chapter 2, the voluntary continuous assessment strands of the program are designed to help teachers align their ongoing classroom assessment activities with the expectations embodied in the accountability strand. Resources are provided to help teachers respond constructively to the demands of the system, improving their students' performance without focusing narrowly on test scores alone as the goals of instruction.

All that being said, serious risks remain that the accountability assessments will weigh too heavily on the curriculum. No matter how comprehensive the set of assessments may be, curricular heterogeneity across the state is likely to diminish, and what is not tested is unlikely to be taught. Most curriculum specialists would agree that the curriculum should be derived from a conception of the goals of education, not constructed around a collection of tasks, no matter how intrinsically valuable each separate task may be. Gardner (1983) argues that school curricula are already skewed toward verbal and quantitative modes of representation, at the expense of other socially valuable domains of intelligence in which different students may excel. From Ben Oldham's comments in chapter 4 concerning the curriculum's heavy emphasis on written communication skills, it appears that the current assessment battery could press the curriculum even further in the verbal/quantitative direction. This seems unfortunate, even paradoxical, given the prominence of "hands-on" or "performance" activities in both KIRIS and contemporary instructional theory. Finally, as Madaus (1988) notes, high-stakes test scores may become the most important goal of education. Something is lost when teachers and students work for grades themselves instead of the intellectual attainments those grades are meant to represent.

In years to come, it will be important that the KIRIS tests continue to change and evolve. The idea of tests worth teaching to is *not* that students are directly taught to perform the assessment tasks themselves, but rather that they are instructed on tasks in some way similar to the assessment tasks. It is difficult to imagine any classroom assessment task, written or hands-on, that could not be reduced to a meaningless rote performance with sufficient training. Teaching *to* the test, but not teaching the test itself, prepares students for the entire domain of tasks from which the actual test tasks are drawn. It follows, however, that teachers and students must know what that domain is like in order to prepare appropriately. In addition, the domain must be appropriately drawn. If it is too broad, instruction will be scattered and ineffective, a game in which teachers gamble on hitting the content tested. If it is too narrow, teaching is easy, but mastery counts for little. Madaus (1988) describes how with any recurrent high-stakes test, a tradition of past examinations develops and, over time, examiners become reluctant to make significant changes from year to year because then teachers will not know what to teach. In other words, he predicts that the domain of test tasks will grow too narrow. If there is too much variation in Kentucky's assessments from year to year, teachers will not be able to catch on or keep up. But the greater risk is that there will be too little variation. Scores will rise, but instruction will become stereotyped, and students who have learned to do well on the particular kinds of items included may do poorly on equally valid items that are testing the same skills in a slightly different way.

Psychometric Challenges

The move to primarily performance-based assessments in KIRIS poses significant technical challenges. The current implementation is state-of-the-art, and early data on the reliability of constructed-response tasks are encouraging. Nonetheless, new technical problems can be anticipated as transitional tests are phased out, more content areas are brought on-line, and the challenges are faced of keeping standards constant over time and across subject areas.

The low reliability (or generalizability) of performance assessments is generally recognized as a serious problem (Dunbar et al., 1991; Linn, 1993; Shavelson et al., 1992). In KIRIS, high reliability has been obtained by restricting high-stakes decision making to the school level (aggregating a lot of student-level information to create a more reliable composite) and by pooling data across 2 years at a time (again doubling the amount of information). Any pressures to use or interpret data at the *individual* level must be resisted until such time as adequate reliability is assured.

Standard setting may prove even more problematical. It was relatively straightforward to establish rules for distinguishing Novice, Apprentice, Proficient, and Distinguished categories of performance in the base year. These categories represent reasoned judgments. Because they are described in terms of the manner of task performance as opposed to abstract qualities of students or predictions about future performance, they appear defensible and unlikely to invite unwarranted interpretations. The challenge now arises, however, of setting equivalent levels on next year's assessment tasks, which may not be of exactly the same difficulty as last year's. The most obvious equating study designs are invalidated by the fact that Kentucky's students may have received instruction on last year's assessment tasks and, in any equating study, next year's tasks would be novel. It follows that, even if tasks from the 2 years were of equal difficulty, a study comparing the performance of equivalent groups of Kentucky students on the two sets of tasks would appear to show that next year's tasks were harder. A related problem arises in establishing standards with comparable meaning in additional subject areas. As Ben Oldham observes, content committees for a given area may have some incentive to establish higher standards to promote allocation of more instructional time to their own disciplines.

Finally, there are technical challenges in combining information across cognitive and noncognitive indicators, across grade levels, and across content areas to arrive at an overall score for a school. Here, details matter a lot. The precise formula adopted will modulate a school's allocations of instructional resources across grade levels and among different student groups, their promotion and retention policies, their assignments of teachers to different grade levels, and many other day-to-day policies. High-stakes testing is a powerful policy instrument. It must be used carefully if it is to work for good and not for ill. The policy makers, educational administrators, technical advisors, and contractors involved in making KIRIS happen must remain alert to its effects, both bad and good, and continue the delicate process of modifying and tuning the system for the benefit of the children of Kentucky. The task is well begun. The nation is watching.

References

Ambach, G. M. (1984). State and local action for education in New York. *Phi Delta Kappan, 66,* 202-204.

Cohen, D. K., & Haney, W. (1980). Minimum competency testing and social policy. In R. M. Jaeger & C. K. Tittle (Eds.), *Minimum competency achievement testing: Motives, models, measures, and consequences* (pp. 5-22). Berkeley, CA: McCutchan.

Cole, N. S. (1988). A realist's appraisal of the prospects for unifying instruction and assessment. In Educational Testing Service, *Assessment in the service of learning* (Proceedings of the 1987 ETS Invitational Conference, pp. 103-117). Princeton, NJ: Educational Testing Service.

Darling-Hammond, L. (1991). The implications of testing policy for educational quality and equality. *Phi Delta Kappan, 73,* 220-225.

Dickey, E. M. (1986). A comparison of advanced placement and college students on a calculus achievement test. *Journal for Research in Mathematics Education, 17,* 140-144.

Dunbar, S. B., Koretz, D. M., & Hoover, H. D. (1991). Quality control in the development and use of performance assessments. *Applied Measurement in Education, 4,* 289-303.

Freeman, J. (1987). The international baccalaureate. *College Board Review, 143,* 4-6, 40.

Gardner, H. (1983). *Frames of mind: The theory of multiple intelligences.* New York: Basic Books.

Glass, G. V. (1978). Matthew Arnold and minimum competence. *Educational Forum, 42,* 139-144.

Godsey, M. (1989). International baccalaureate of the Americas: A comparative approach. *New England Journal of History, 46*(2), 21-34.

Haertel, E. H. (1989). Student achievement tests as tools of educational policy: Practices and consequences. In B. Gifford (Ed.), *Test policy and test performance: Education, language, and culture* (pp. 25-50). Boston: Kluwer.

Herr, N. E. (1991). The influence of program format on the professional development of science teachers: Teacher perceptions of AP and honors science courses. *Science Teacher, 75,* 619-629.

Jaeger, R. M. (1991). Legislative perspectives on statewide testing: Goals, hopes, and desires. *Phi Delta Kappan, 73*, 239-242.

Koretz, D. M., Madaus, G. F., Haertel, E. H., & Beaton, A. E. (1992, February 19). *National educational standards and testing: A response to the recommendations of the National Council on Education Standards and Testing* (Invited joint testimony presented by Daniel M. Koretz before the Subcommittee on Elementary, Secondary, and Vocational Education, Committee on Education and Labor, U.S. House of Representatives). (Available as Report No. CT-100 from RAND Corporation, Washington, DC)

Linn, R. L. (1993). Educational assessment: Expanded expectations and challenges. *Educational Evaluation and Policy Analysis, 15*, 1-16.

Madaus, G. F. (1985). Test scores as administrative mechanisms in educational policy. *Phi Delta Kappan, 66*, 611-617.

Madaus, G. F. (1988). The influence of testing on the curriculum. In L. N. Tanner (Ed.), *Critical issues in curriculum* (Eighty-seventh yearbook of the National Society for the Study of Education, pt. 1, pp. 83-121). Chicago: University of Chicago Press.

McDill, E. L., Natriello, G., & Pallas, A. M. (1985). Raising standards and retaining students: The impact of the reform recommendations on potential dropouts. *Review of Educational Research, 55*, 415-433.

Resnick, L. B., & Resnick, D. P. (1992). Assessing the thinking curriculum: New tools for educational reform. In B. Gifford & M. C. O'Connor (Eds.), *Changing assessments: Alternative views of aptitude, achievement, and instruction* (pp. 37-75). Boston: Kluwer.

Shavelson, R. J., Baxter, G. P., & Pine, J. (1992). Performance assessments: Political rhetoric and measurement reality. *Educational Researcher, 21*(4), 22-27.

Shepard, L. A. (1991). Will national tests improve student learning? *Phi Delta Kappan, 73*, 232-238.

Valentine, J. A. (1987). *The college board and the school curriculum. A history of the college board's influence on the substance and standards of American education, 1900-1980.* New York: College Entrance Examination Board. (ERIC Document Reproduction Service No. ED 285 443)

Whelan, R. (1989). A high school-college cooperative program in Advanced Placement physics laboratory. *Physics Teacher, 27,* 182-184.

Wiggins, G. (1992). Creating tests worth taking. *Educational Leadership, 49*(8), 26-33.

Wolf, D., Bixby, J., Glenn, J., III, & Gardner, H. (1991). To use their minds well: Investigating new forms of student assessment. *Review of Research in Education, 17,* 31-74.

Wolf, D. P., LeMahieu, P. G., & Eresh, J. (1992). Good measure: Assessment as a tool for educational reform. *Educational Leadership, 49*(8), 8-13.

APPENDIX A

Assessment and Accountability Legislation

EDUCATIONAL IMPROVEMENT

158.645 Capacities required of students in public education system

The General Assembly recognizes that public education involves shared responsibilities. State government, local communities, parents, students, and school employees must work together to create an efficient public school system. Parents and students must assist schools with efforts to assure student attendance, preparation for school, and involvement in learning. The cooperation of all involved is necessary to assure that desired outcomes are achieved. It is the intent of the General Assembly to create a system of public education which shall allow and assist all students to acquire the following capacities:

(1) Communication skills necessary to function in a complex and changing civilization;

(2) Knowledge to make economic, social, and political choices;

(3) Understanding of governmental processes as they affect the community, the state, and the nation;

(4) Sufficient self-knowledge and knowledge of his mental and physical wellness;

(5) Sufficient grounding in the arts to enable each student to appreciate his or her cultural and historical heritage;

(6) Sufficient preparation to choose and pursue his life's work intelligently; and

(7) Skills to enable him to compete favorably with students in other states.

HISTORY: 1990 c 476, § 2, eff. 7-13-90

CROSS-REFERENCES

Office of education accountability, goal of system of schools, school district audits, 7.410

Required adoption of schools councils for school-based decision making, 160.345

NOTES ON DECISIONS AND OPINIONS

790 SW(2d) 186 (Ky 1989), Rose v Council for Better Education, Inc. The essential and minimal characteristics of an "efficient" system of common schools are (1) the establishment, maintenance, and funding of the common schools solely by the general assembly; (2) common schools shall be free and available to all Kentucky children; (3) common schools shall be substantially uniform throughout the state; (4) equal educational opportunities shall be afforded all children in the state regardless of place of residence or economic circumstances; (5) common schools shall be monitored by the General Assembly to assure they are operated without waste, duplication, mismanagement, or political influence; (6) the premise for the existence of common schools is that all children in Kentucky have a constitutional right to an adequate education which has as its goal the development of basic academic, social, and vocational capacities; and (7) the general assembly shall provide funding sufficient to provide each child in Kentucky with an adequate education.

158.6451　Council on School Performance Standards; development of goals for Commonwealth's schools; model curriculum framework

(1) Upon July 13, 1990, the Council on School Performance Standards established by Executive Order 89-151 shall be reconvened by the chairman to frame the following six (6) goals for the schools of the Commonwealth in measurable terms which define the outcomes expected of students:

(a) Schools shall expect a high level of achievement of all students.

(b) Schools shall develop their students' ability to:

1. Use basic communication and mathematics skills for purposes and situations they will encounter throughout their lives;

2. Apply core concepts and principles from mathematics, the sciences, the arts, the humanities, social studies, and practical-living studies to situations they will encounter throughout their lives;

3. Become a self-sufficient individual;

4. Become responsible members of a family, work group, or community, including demonstrating effectiveness in community service;

5. Think and solve problems in school situations and in a variety of situations they will encounter in life; and

6. Connect and integrate experiences and new knowledge from all subject matter fields with what they have previously learned and build on past learning experiences to acquire new information through various media sources.

(c) Schools shall increase their students' rate of school attendance.

(d) Schools shall reduce their students' dropout and retention rates.

(e) Schools shall reduce physical and mental health barriers to learning.

(f) Schools shall be measured on the proportion of students who make a successful transition to work, postsecondary education, and the military.

(2) The Council on School Performance Standards shall employ necessary staff and shall be attached to the Department of Education for administrative purposes. Members of the council and its committees may receive reimbursement of actual expenses for attending meetings and may be reimbursed for other actual and necessary expenses incurred in the performance of their duties authorized by the council. The expenses shall be paid out of the appropriation for the council.

(3) The Council on School Performance Standards shall establish a number of committees with statewide representation of certified personnel to frame the goals in measurable terms which specify the expected outcomes. The council shall make periodic progress reports and a final report by December 1, 1991, to the Governor, the State Board for Elementary and Secondary Education, and the Legislative Research Commission. After submitting its final report the council shall cease to exist. The State Board for Elementary and Secondary Education shall adopt the goals of the council.

(4) By July 1, 1993, the State Board for Elementary and Secondary Education shall disseminate to local school districts and schools a model curriculum framework which is directly tied to the goals, outcomes, and assessment strategies developed pursuant to this section and KRS 158.645 and 158.6453. The framework shall provide direction to local districts and schools as they develop their curriculum. The framework shall identify teaching and assessment strategies, instructional material resources, ideas on how to incorporate the resources of the community, a directory of model teaching sites, and alternative ways of using school time.

HISTORY: 1990 c 476, § 3, eff. 7-13-90

CROSS-REFERENCES

Adoption of administrative regulations by state board for elementary and secondary education, 156.160

158.6453 Assessment of achievement of goals; development of state-wide assessment program; publication of annual performance report by districts

(1) The State Board for Elementary and Secondary Education shall be responsible for creating and implementing a statewide, primarily performance-based assessment program to ensure school accountability for student achievement of the goals set forth in KRS 158.645. The program shall be implemented as early as the 1993-94 school year but no later than the 1995-96 school year. The board shall also be responsible for administering an interim testing program to assess student skills in reading, mathematics, writing, science, and social studies in Grades four (4), eight (8), and twelve (12). The tests shall be designed to provide the state with national comparisons and shall be the same as, or similar to, those used by the National Assessment of Educational Progress. The interim testing program shall begin during the 1991-92 school year and shall be administered to a sample of students representative of each school and the state as a whole. The test scores shall be used, along with other factors described in KRS 158.6451, to establish a baseline for determining school success during the 1993-94 school year.

(2) Upon July 13, 1990, the state board shall contract with three (3) or more authorities in the field of performance assessment to design the specifications for the interim and full-scale statewide assessment development effort. The bid specifications shall include requirements that the successful bidder:

(a) Be a consultant to the Council on School Performance Standards as it develops the educational outcomes expected of students;

(b) Direct the development of the interim and full-scale assessment program; and

(c) Direct the development of the formula to be used to determine successful schools pursuant to KRS 158.6455. The assessment authorities shall review the bids and make a recommendation to the board. The authorities shall have no pecuniary interest with the successful bidder.

(3) In addition to statewide testing for the purpose of determining school success, the board shall have the responsibility of assisting local school districts and schools in developing and using continuous assessment strategies needed to assure student progress.

(4) By October 1 of each year, local boards of education shall publish in the newspaper with the largest circulation in the county an annual performance report on district accomplishments and activities pertaining to performance goals including, but not limited to, retention rates and student performance, the districts' goals for the succeeding year, and other items as may be set forth in State Board for Elementary and Secondary Education administrative regulations.

HISTORY: 1990 c 476, § 4, eff. 7-13-90

158.6455 Determination of and rewards to successful schools; school improvement plan for schools not meeting goals; "schools in crisis"; appeals of performance judgments

It is the intent of the General Assembly that schools succeed with all students and receive the appropriate consequences in proportion to that success.

(1) The State Board for Elementary and Secondary Education shall promulgate administrative regulations to establish a system of determining successful schools and dispensing appropriate rewards. The system shall be based on the following:

(a) A school shall be the unit of measure to determine success;

(b) School success shall be determined by measuring a school's improvement over a two (2) year period;

(c) A school shall be rewarded for an increased proportion of successful students, including those students who are at risk of school failure;

(d) A threshold level for school improvement shall be established by the board to determine the amount of success needed for a school to receive a reward. The threshold definition shall establish the percentage of increase required in a school's percentage of successful students as compared to a school's present proportion of successful students, with consideration given to the fact that a school closest to having one hundred percent (100%) successful students will have a lower percentage increase required;

(e) Rewards shall be given to the school on behalf of the full-time, part-time, and itinerant instructional staff of a school who generate the reward when the school achieves at least one percent (1%) gain over its threshold as defined in paragraph (d) of this subsection. Substitute teachers shall not be used in calculating the reward;

(f) Rewards shall be calculated by applying the percentage set by the General Assembly in the biennial budget to the current annual salary of each certified staff person employed in the school on the last working day of the year of the reward. The reward for part-time and itinerant staff shall be calculated for the proportion of time spent in the school. In determining the percentage to be applied to a school for calculation of the rewards for the school's staff, consideration shall be given to the fact that schools already having a high percentage of successful students shall have a lower requirement for a percentage increase in its number of successful students. The staff person's identity in connection to his share of the reward shall be maintained when his share of the reward is deposited to the school's account;

(g) The certified staff members shall by majority rule collectively decide on the ways the reward funds shall be spent. Each individual staff person shall use the amount he earned in accordance with the decisions made by the total staff. Rewards shall not be added to a staff person's base salary and shall not be defined as compensation for retirement purposes under KRS 161.220(10); and

(h) The Department of Education shall send the school's reward to the local district office for transmittal to the school.

(2) The State Board for Elementary and Secondary Education, after adopting the goals of the Council on School Performance Standards and determining the definition of a successful student, shall adopt by administrative regulation the formula to be used to determine successful schools. The formula shall be a calculus of factors which reflect the school outcomes described in KRS 158.6451.

(3) A school that does not reach its threshold level as defined in paragraph (d) of subsection (1) of this section but maintains the previous proportion of successful students shall be required to develop a school improvement plan and shall be eligible to receive funds from the school improvement fund pursuant to KRS 158.805. A school that does not reach its threshold level but maintains the previous proportion of successful students after the second biennial review shall be required to meet the provisions of subsection (4) of this section.

(4) A school in which the proportion of successful students declines by less than five percent (5%) shall be required to develop a school improvement plan, shall be eligible to receive funds from the school improvement fund, and shall have one (1) or more Kentucky distinguished educators assigned to the school to carry out the duties as described in KRS 158.782. If the school does not meet its original threshold after the next biennial review, the school shall be subject to the requirements of subsection (5) of this section.

(5) A school in which the proportion of successful students declines by five percent (5%) or more shall be declared by the State Board for

Elementary and Secondary Education to be a "school in crisis." When a school is declared to be a "school in crisis," the following actions shall be required:

(a) The full-time and part-time certified staff of that school shall be placed on probation;

(b) The principal shall immediately notify the students' parents of the students' right to transfer to a successful school, with procedures for initiating the request;

(c) Within thirty (30) days after the declaration by the state board under this subsection or no later than thirty (30) days before the start of the next school year, whichever is later, any student in that school may request and shall be allowed to transfer to a successful school as determined under the provisions of subsection (2) of this section. The superintendent shall select the receiving successful school in the home district or make arrangements with a neighboring district. If two (2) districts cannot agree, the superintendent of the student's resident district shall request the State Board for Elementary and Secondary Education to resolve the issue and make a decision on the placement of the student within thirty (30) days of the request. The board of the district in which the student resides shall be responsible for all tuition and transportation costs incurred as a result of a student transferring from a "school in crisis" to a successful school. If a decline in student enrollment causes overstaffing at the "school in crisis," personnel shall be reduced or transferred pursuant to KRS 161.760 and 161.800.

(d) One (1) or more Kentucky distinguished educators shall be assigned to the school by the commissioner of education to carry out the duties as described in KRS 158.782. Notwithstanding any other statute to the contrary, at the end of six (6) months, the Kentucky distinguished educator shall evaluate and make a recommendation to the superintendent regarding the retention, dismissal, or transfer of each full-time and part-time certified staff member. Recommendations for transfer shall conform to any employer-employee bargained contract which is in effect. Recommendations for dismissal shall be binding on the superintendent who shall notify the staff member pursuant to KRS 161.790. This evaluation process shall continue every six (6) months until the school is no longer a "school in crisis" as determined by the State Board for Elementary and Secondary Education; and

(e) The school shall be required to develop a school improvement plan and shall be eligible to receive funds from the school improvement fund.

(6) The State Board for Elementary and Secondary Education shall develop a system of rewards and sanctions for certified staff who are not

assigned to a school in a local school district. The system shall be analogous to the system described in subsections (1) through (5) of this section. Rewards shall be given to non-school-based staff when the district's proportion of successful students increases above a threshold adopted by the state board and comparable to the threshold adopted for schools. Sanctions shall be imposed when the proportion of successful students in the district declines in the same proportion used to determine school sanctions under subsections (3), (4), and (5) of this section. A school district that does not meet its threshold shall be required to develop a district improvement plan defined in KRS 158.650.

(7) A school district in which the proportion of successful students declines by five percent (5%) or more shall be assigned one (1) or more Kentucky distinguished educators to assist the system, evaluate personnel, and notwithstanding any other statute to the contrary, make personnel recommendations every six (6) months on retention, dismissal, or transfer. Personnel recommendations shall be made to the superintendent. Recommendations on the superintendent's status shall be made to the local board of education. If the recommendation is to terminate the superintendent, the board shall terminate the contract pursuant to KRS 160.350. If a district has a declining proportion of successful students for two (2) consecutive biennial assessment periods, the district shall be declared an education development district pursuant to KRS 158.685 and the board members and the superintendent shall be removed under the provisions of KRS 156.132 and 156.136.

(8) The State Board for Elementary and Secondary Education shall adopt administrative regulations to establish a process whereby a school shall be allowed to appeal a performance judgment which it considers grossly unfair. The state board may adjust a performance judgment on appeal when evidence of highly unusual circumstances warrants the conclusion that the performance judgment is based on fraud or a mistake in computations, is arbitrary, is lacking any reasonable basis, or when there are significant new circumstances occurring during the biennial assessment period which are beyond the control of the school.

HISTORY: 1990 c 476, § 5, eff. 7-13-90

CROSS-REFERENCES

Superintendent of schools: termination after recommendation of Kentucky distinguished educator, 160.350

Termination of teacher's contract by board, charges, 161.790

158.650   Definitions for KRS 158.680 to 158.710

As used in KRS 158.680 to 158.710, unless the context otherwise requires:

(1) "Department" means the Department of Education;

(2) "Competencies" means the possession of skills, knowledge, and understandings to the degree they can be demonstrated or measured;

(3) "Performance goals" means expected student and school district outcomes as approved by the State Board for Elementary and Secondary Education;

(4) "Interim performance goal" means the specified amount of improvement the district shall achieve toward meeting the performance goal agreed upon in the district improvement plan;

(5) "Process goals" means systematic and orderly procedures, including specific actions and time frames to be followed in achieving performance goals;

(6) "Standards" means acceptable levels of attainment school districts shall meet in student, program, service, and operational performance as established in administrative regulations adopted by the State Board for Elementary and Secondary Education;

(7) "Educationally deficient school district" means a school district which does not meet minimum standards in student, program, service, or operational performance;

(8) "Education development district" means an educationally deficient district which fails to meet all process goals or to achieve all interim performance goals according to the time lines established in the district improvement plan;

(9) "Annual performance report" means the report published annually by each local board of education that presents the district's performance with regard to performance goals as established by State Board for Elementary and Secondary Education administrative regulations; and

(10) "District improvement plan" means the plan developed by a local school district in consultation with the Department of Education, that establishes the process goals and time lines for correcting identified deficiencies in the achievement of performance goals and the interim performance goals. The plan shall be approved by the local board of education and the State Board for Elementary and Secondary Education.

HISTORY: 1990 c 476, § 8, eff. 7-13-90; 1988 c 357, § 1; 1984 c 347, § 1, c 65, § 1; 1982 c 13, § 1; 1978 c 151, § 2

158.660 to 158.670 Intent and purpose; basic skills development regulations; department to administer Educational Improvement Act; administrative regulations—Repealed

HISTORY: 1990 c 476, § 616, eff. 7-13-90; 1988 c 357, §2.3; 1986 c 57, § 1; 1984 c 347, §2, 4, c 65, § 2, c 397, § 4; 1982 c 13, § 2; 1978 c 151, § 3, 4

158.680 State Advisory Committee for Educational Improvement

There shall be appointed by the Governor a State Advisory Committee for Educational Improvement in accordance with the following:

(1) The State Advisory Committee for Educational Improvement shall be eighteen (18) members broadly representative of citizens, parents, teachers, and administrators. Their principal duties shall be to advise the Governor, the State Board for Elementary and Secondary Education, and the department on the implementation of the provisions of KRS 158.650 to 158.710 and KRS 158.6453 and 158.6455.

(2) All members shall be voting members appointed by the Governor and shall serve terms of four (4) years, except that the original appointments will be made as follows:

(a) Five (5) members for four (4)-year terms;

(b) Five (5) members for three (3)-year terms;

(c) Four (4) members for two (2)-year terms; and

(d) Four (4) members for a one (1)-year term.

(3) The State Advisory Committee for Educational Improvement shall elect a chairman annually from its membership;

(4) The members shall be remunerated for actual and necessary expenses incurred while attending meetings of the State Advisory Committee for Educational Improvement or while serving in the capacity as representative of the State Advisory Committee for Educational Improvement.

(5) The State Advisory Committee for Educational Improvement shall meet at least three (3) times each year at times and places as it determines by resolution.

HISTORY: 1990 c 476, § 9, eff. 7-13-90; 1988 c 357, § 4; 1978 c 151, § 5

CROSS-REFERENCES

Educational Improvement Act, duties and functions, 704 KAR 3:005

158.685 Standards of student, program, service, and operational performance to be established; educationally deficient school district action to eliminate deficiency; education development district

(1) The State Board for Elementary and Secondary Education shall adopt administrative regulations establishing standards which school districts shall meet in student, program, service, and operational performance. The State Board for Elementary and Secondary Education shall promulgate regulations establishing operational performance standards by January 1, 1991. These standards shall become effective on July 1, 1991.

(2) The State Board for Elementary and Secondary Education shall declare a school district to be educationally deficient when, in any school year, the district fails to meet minimum student, program, service, or operational performance standards.

(3) The chief state school officer shall provide consultation and assistance to any school district which has been declared educationally deficient by the State Board for Elementary and Secondary Education. The school district shall be provided consultation and guidance relative to programs, services, finances, personnel, and any other areas where appropriate changes would be reasonably calculated to eliminate or alleviate the deficiency and in developing and implementing a district improvement plan pursuant to KRS 158.710. The changes may include improved personnel administration, more efficient management practices, and other administrative and academic actions to improve the local district's performance. The Department of Education shall submit to the local board and superintendent a list of the services and technical assistance the department shall provide. The services listed may include activities and programs offered for the improvement of all districts. The list of services shall be attached to the district improvement plan when it is submitted to the State Board for Elementary and Secondary Education for approval.

(4) Failure by an educationally deficient school district to meet the process goals, interim performance goals, or time lines set in the district improvement plan shall constitute grounds for removal of the superintendent and local board members from office and this action shall be initiated by the chief state school officer pursuant to KRS 156.132 and 156.136. The district shall also be declared an education development district. The State Board for Elementary and Secondary Education shall appoint the members of the district's board of education which shall have all the powers, duties, and responsibilities of an elected board, except as provided in this

section. The appointed members shall serve a four (4)-year term or until the district qualifies for an elected board and the duly elected members have taken office, whichever occurs first. When a new superintendent of schools is selected by the local board, the chief state school officer shall approve the selection before the appointment shall become official. The local board shall revise the district improvement plan with the assistance of the Department of Education. The Department of Education shall continue to provide the district consultation and assistance pursuant to subsection (3) of this section. Local board elections shall resume in the first even-numbered year following two (2) consecutive years of meeting the performance standards set by the State Board for Elementary and Secondary Education. This section shall not create a statutory cause of action for educational malpractice by students, their parents or guardians.

HISTORY: 1990 c 476, § 10, eff. 7-13-90; 1988 c 357, § 5; 1984 c 347, § 3

CROSS-REFERENCES

Professional program for certified personnel; master professional development plan exempt, 156.095

158.690 and 158.700 Assessment and testing program; publication of test results; specific duties of department—Repealed

HISTORY: 1990 c 476, § 616, eff. 7-13-90; 1988 c 357, § 6, 7; 1986 c 341, § 1; 1984 c 397, § 1, c 347, § 5, 6, c 66, § 1; 1982 c 13, § 3, 4; 1978 c 151, § 6, 7

NOTES ON DECISIONS AND OPINIONS

OAG 86-72. A school district's annual performance report required pursuant to KRS 150.690 cannot be published in a newspaper that is distributed free; publication of the report is governed by KRS 424.120, relating to qualification of newspapers for legal notices. (Annotation from former KRS 158.690.)

OAG 84-374. A "common school" is a school taught in a district laid out by authority of the school laws. There are 120 county plus 60 independent common school districts in the Commonwealth. The schools at Fort Knox, Fort Campbell, and Madison Model are not public common schools. The scope of the statutes dealing with testing for educational improvements covers only the present 180 public common school districts. (Annotation from former KRS 158.690.)

158.710 Responsibilities and functions of educationally deficient districts and education development districts; plans required; reports required

Each educationally deficient district and education development district shall assume the following responsibilities and functions in implementing the provisions of KRS 158.680 to 158.710:

(1) The district shall develop a plan to improve the education of all students enrolled in preschool and the primary program through grade twelve (12). In developing the plan and prior to approval by the local board of education, the district shall involve local citizens, parents, students, teachers, and administrators. The district, pursuant to KRS 158.685, shall involve Department of Education consultants in the development of the plan;

(2) Educationally deficient districts and education development districts pursuant to KRS 158.685 shall submit a plan each year, or more frequently if ordered by the State Board for Elementary and Secondary Education, listing new process goals, the interim performance goals, and time lines until the deficiency has been eliminated;

(3) Local school personnel shall ascertain areas of strength and areas needing improvement in the school program as revealed by the test results and other student assessments and with the advice and counsel of the representatives mentioned in subsection (1) of this section, shall develop appropriate programs to address educational areas needing improvement for all students in preschool and the primary program through grade twelve (12);

(4) The district improvement plan developed and submitted to the department shall include the following:

(a) Performance goals or interim performance goals;

(b) Product goals;

(c) A list of individuals, by occupation, or groups involved in developing the plan;

(d) The areas of needed improvement as revealed by the district assessment results;

(e) A list of priorities for program implementation;

(f) The objectives and activities deemed appropriate and necessary for alleviating the observed educational areas of needed improvement;

(g) A calendar of events and time line, for implementation;

(h) A brief report, each succeeding year, or more frequently if required by the State Board for Elementary and Secondary Education, after submission of the initial plan, of the program status and progress made in areas of needed improvement.

(5) The district improvement plan shall be coordinated with the master staff development plan and the Department of Education shall provide technical assistance in the planning, implementation, and evaluation of this coordination.

(6) Effective June 30, 1996, KRS 158.650 to 158.710 shall become null and void.

HISTORY: 1990 c 476, § 11, eff. 7-13-90; 1988 c 357, § 8; 1984 c 347, § 7; 1982 c 13, § 5; 1978 c 151, § 8

CROSS-REFERENCES

Educational Improvement Act, duties and functions, 704 KAR 3:005

Accountability Index Worksheets

Computing a School's
Accountability Index and Threshold

This worksheet provides a sample set of data for a hypothetical high school. Use these data and the step-by-step procedure outlined to compute the high school's baseline accountability index and threshold.

Step 1: Combine Matrix and Common Data

The first step in computing a school's accountability index is to average the common open-ended and matrix-sampled data from the transitional test. Fifty percent of the weight is given to common items and 50% to matrix-sampled items. For example, using the sample data from Table B-1, 0.46% of the students are classified as "distinguished" based on the common mathematics items and 2.11% of the students are classified as "distinguished" based on the matrix-sampled mathematics items; therefore, the average is 1.2850%, meaning that 1.2850% of the students are classified as "distinguished" in mathematics.

Using the sample data in Table B-1, compute the average for social studies. Reading, mathematics, and science are computed for you. Record each average in Table B-2 rounded to the nearest ten thousandth (4 decimal places).

Step 2: Combine Transitional Test Results and
Performance Events

The second step in computing a school's accountability index is to combine the results of the transitional test (Table B-2) and the performance events (Table B-3). These two components are combined giving 80% of the weight to transitional tests and 20% to performance events. Using the distinguished category in mathematics, an example of the computation involved in this step follows: $(1.2850 \times .80) + (2.06 \times .20) = 1.4400$.

The computation for mathematics and science is completed for you. Combine the social studies data by using working Table A to multiply transitional data (Table B-2) times .80 and working Table B to multiply performance events data (Table B-3) times .20. Add the data in corresponding cells from working Tables A and B and record results in Table B-4 to the nearest ten thousandth (4 decimal places).

Step 3: Compute Cognitive Index for Each Content Area

Each of the performance levels has been assigned the following point values: *Novice* = 0; *Apprentice* = 2; *Proficient* = 5; *Distinguished* = 7. On a scale of 0 to 5, where 5 equals 100% or 1.00, each unit must be worth .20; therefore, an equivalent scale is derived in working Table C.

Using the mathematics data from Table B-4 as an example, our hypothetical high school has 52.5660% of its students scoring at the novice level, 38.7820% at the apprentice level, 7.2120% at the proficient level, and 1.4400% at the distinguished level. The school would receive an accountability index in mathematics of 24.7408; that is, $(52.5660 \times 0) + (38.7820 \times .40) + (7.2120 \times 1.00) + (1.4400 \times 1.40)$. Using the weights from working Table C, the sample writing portfolio data from Table B-5, and the reading, mathematics, science, and social studies data from Table B-4, compute the cognitive index for social studies using working Tables D and E and Table B-6 to record results. Round each content area accountability index to the nearest ten thousandth (4 decimal places). Reading, mathematics, science, and writing have been computed for you.

Step 4: Compute the Noncognitive Index

The approved weighted values for each noncognitive indicator at Grades 4, 8, and 12 are given in Table B-7.

Two of the indicators—attendance and transition—are reported in positive terms; that is, a high percentage indicates a high degree of success; however, the indicators retention and dropout must be subtracted from 100 in order to have values that are consistent with attendance and transition. For example, if the retention rate is 6.07%, it must be converted to 93.93%. This converted value is then multiplied by the retention rate weight at Grade 12; that is, $93.93 \times .05 = 4.6965$. The noncognitive index is computed by multiplying the reported value (converted value for retention and dropout) for each indicator times its weight. Finally, these products are added to get the noncognitive index.

Using the weights from Table B-7 and the sample data from Table B-8, compute the noncognitive index and record in Table B-9. The computation for attendance, retention, and transition is completed for you. The noncognitive index should be rounded to the nearest ten thousandth (4 decimal places).

Step 5: Combine Cognitive and Noncognitive Indexes

In this step, the six indexes—reading, mathematics, science, social studies, writing, and noncognitive index— are combined into a single overall accountability index. This overall accountability index is the school's baseline and is calculated by simple averaging. Use the results from Tables B-6 and B-9 to find the baseline accountability index and record in Table B-10. Round the overall accountability index to the nearest tenth.

Step 6: Computing the Threshold

The procedure for calculating a school's threshold is to first compute the distance between the school's baseline and 100; that is, the gap between where a school is and where it ultimately wants to be. Second, divide this number by 10 and round to the nearest tenth. This result represents the amount of growth expected for the given accountability period. Third, add the "expected growth" to the baseline. This sum represents the school's threshold. For example, if a school's baseline is 40, the gap is 60 (i.e., $100 - 40 = 60$). Sixty divided by 10 equals 6. Forty plus 6 equals 46 for the school's threshold.

Using the baseline accountability index calculated in Table B-10, compute the school's threshold and record in Table B-11.

The baseline accountability index should be 39.5 and the threshold should be 45.6.

Table B-1. Percentage of Students at Each Performance Level (Transitional Test, Based on Hypothetical Data)

Performance Category	Reading	Math	Science	Social Studies
Common open-ended transitional test				
Novice	42.02	56.28	33.18	46.51
Apprentice	51.63	37.20	63.98	44.91
Proficient	5.60	6.06	2.35	8.56
Distinguished	0.75	0.46	0.49	0.02
Matrix open-ended transitional test				
Novice	43.77	49.89	31.06	42.62
Apprentice	49.69	40.00	65.73	46.71
Proficient	5.30	8.00	2.15	8.67
Distinguished	1.24	2.11	1.06	2.00

Table B-2. Percentage of Students at Each Performance Level, Matrix and Common Data Combined

Performance Category	Reading	Math	Science
Novice	42.8950	53.0850	32.1200
Apprentice	50.6600	38.6000	64.8550
Proficient	5.4500	7.0300	2.2500
Distinguished	0.9950	1.2850	0.7750

Table B-3. Percentage of Students at Each Performance Level
(Performance Events, Based on Hypothetical Data)

Performance Category	Reading	Math	Science	Social Studies
Novice	50.49	39.70	49.81	
Apprentice	39.51	45.77	44.49	
Proficient	7.94	10.05	4.10	
Distinguished	2.06	4.48	1.60	

Working Table A. Transitional Test x .80

Performance Category	Math	Science	Social Studies
Novice	42.4680	25.6960	
Apprentice	30.8800	51.8840	
Proficient	5.6240	1.8000	
Distinguished	1.0280	0.6200	

Working Table B. Performance Events x .20

Performance Category	Math	Science	Social Studies
Novice	10.0980	7.9400	
Apprentice	7.9020	9.1540	
Proficient	1.5880	2.0100	
Distinguished	0.4120	0.8960	

Table B-4. Combination of Transitional Test Results and Performance Events

Performance Category	Reading	Math	Science
Novice	42.8950	52.5660	33.6360
Apprentice	50.6600	38.7820	61.0380
Proficient	5.4500	7.2120	3.8100
Distinguished	0.9950	1.4400	1.5160

Table B-5. Percentage of Students at Each Performance Level (Writing Portfolio, Based on Hypothetical Data)

Performance Category	Writing Portfolio
Novice	33.96
Apprentice	50.14
Proficient	11.99
Distinguished	3.91

Working Table C. Point Values Assigned Different Performance Categories

Performance Category	Point Value
Novice	0.00
Apprentice	0.40
Proficient	1.00
Distinguished	1.40

Working Table D. Calculations by Performance Categories

Performance Category	Reading	Math	Science	Social Studies	Writing
Novice	0×42.8950	0×52.5660	0×33.6360	$0 \times$	0×33.96
Apprentice	$.40 \times 50.6600$	$.40 \times 38.7820$	$.40 \times 61.038$	$.40 \times$	$.40 \times 50.14$
Proficient	1.00×5.4500	1.00×7.2120	1.00×3.810	$1.00 \times$	1.00×11.99
Distinguished	1.40×0.9950	1.40×1.4400	1.40×1.516	$1.40 \times$	1.40×3.91

Working Table E. Computing the Cognitive Index for Each Content Area

Performance Category	Reading	Math	Science	Social Studies	Writing
Novice	0.0000	0.0000	0.0000		0.000
Apprentice	20.2640	15.5128	24.4152		20.056
Proficient	5.4500	7.2120	3.8100		11.990
Distinguished	1.3930	2.0160	2.1224		5.474
Accountability index	27.1070	24.7408	30.3476		37.520

Table B-6. Accountability Index for Each Content Area

Content Area	Accountability Index
Reading	27.1070
Math	24.7408
Science	30.3476
Social studies	
Writing	37.5200

Table B-7. Approved Weighted Values for Each Noncognitive Indicator at Grades 4, 8, and 12 (in percentages)

Noncognitive Indicator	Weight		
	Grade 4	Grade 8	Grade 12
Attendance	80	40	20.0
Retention	20	40	5.0
Dropout	n.a.	20	37.5
Transition	n.a.	n.a.	37.5
Barriers	0	0	0.0

Table B-8. Percentages of Students in Various Noncognitive
Indicators (Based on Hypothetical Data)

Noncognitive Indicator	Percentage
Attendance rate	93.06
Retention rate	6.07
Dropout rate	7.52
Transition rate	85.11

Table B-9. Computing the Noncognitive Index

Indicator	Reported Value	Converted Value	Weight	Weight Times Value
Attendance rate	93.06	93.0600	0.200	18.6120
Retention rate	6.07	93.9300	0.050	4.6965
Dropout rate	7.52	92.4800	0.375	
Transition rate 85.11	85.1100	0.375	31.9163	
Noncognitive index (sum of "weight times value" column				

Table B-10. Baseline Accountability Index: Combining
Cognitive and Noncognitive Indices

Indicator	Index
Reading	27.1070
Math	24.7408
Science	30.3476
Social studies	
Writing	37.5200
Noncognitive index	
Sum	
Accountability index (sum/6)	

Table B-11. Computing the Threshold

Baseline accountability index (from Table B-10)	39.5
Gap (100 minus baseline accountability index)	60.5
Expected growth (gap divided by 10 or 10% of gap)	6.05
Threshold (baseline accountability index plus expected growth)	45.6

Accountability Index Baseline Summary

Percentage of Students at Each Performance Level

	Grade 4				Grade 8				Grade 12			
	Reading	Mathematics	Science	Social Studies	Reading	Mathematics	Science	Social Studies	Reading	Mathematics	Science	Social Studies
Novice	45	59	48	34	16	57	56	34	42	45	33	42
Apprentice	45	30	43	52	69	23	36	49	45	43	61	44
Proficient	3	4	3	7	8	10	1	9	9	8	4	10
Distinguished	0	2	0	0	0	3	0	0	1	2	0	1
Non-tested	6	6	6	6	8	8	8	8	3	2	2	3

Performance Level Percentages Reported by Gender

		Grade 4				Grade 8				Grade 12			
		Reading	Mathematics	Science	Social Studies	Reading	Mathematics	Science	Social Studies	Reading	Mathematics	Science	Social Studies
MALE	Novice	54	65	54	42	23	63	64	42	50	48	35	47
MALE	Apprentice	44	30	43	53	72	24	35	51	42	42	60	43
MALE	Proficient	2	3	3	6	5	10	1	8	7	9	5	10
MALE	Distinguished	0	2	0	0	0	3	0	0	1	2	0	1
FEMALE	Novice	41	60	49	31	10	59	56	31	36	44	31	40
FEMALE	Apprentice	54	34	48	60	78	27	43	56	51	46	65	48
FEMALE	Proficient	5	4	3	9	12	11	1	12	12	8	4	12
FEMALE	Distinguished	0	2	0	0	1	3	0	1	1	2	0	1

Performance Level Percentages Reported by Ethnic Group

		Grade 4				Grade 8				Grade 12			
		Reading	Mathematics	Science	Social Studies	Reading	Mathematics	Science	Social Studies	Reading	Mathematics	Science	Social Studies
WHITE	Novice	47	61	50	35	16	59	59	35	42	45	31	42
WHITE	Apprentice	47	33	47	56	75	26	40	54	47	45	63	46
WHITE	Proficient	4	4	3	8	9	11	1	10	10	9	5	11
WHITE	Distinguished	0	2	0	0	0	3	0	0	1	2	0	1
NON-WHITE	Novice	55	75	65	44	23	77	73	47	56	58	46	55
NON-WHITE	Apprentice	43	22	34	51	71	17	27	47	38	36	51	38
NON-WHITE	Proficient	2	2	1	5	5	5	0	6	6	5	3	7
NON-WHITE	Distinguished	0	1	0	0	0	1	0	0	0	1	0	0

*Percents may not add to 100 due to rounding.